In Wartime Finland
Memories of a World War II Childhood

In Wartime Finland
Memories of a World War II Childhood

Hilja Hautamaa Nast

Translated by Richard Impola

North Star Press of St. Cloud, Inc.

9|07

Acknowledgments

Excerpt on page 14 from *Prayer* - President Roosevelt
Flag Day Speech, June 14, 1942. Copyright © 1942 Stephen
Vincent Benet. Copyright renewed in 1970 by Thomas C.
Benet, Rachel Benet Lewis, and Stephanie Benet Mahin.
Reprinted by permission of Brandt & Brandt Literary
Agents, Inc.

All Artwork by Elisa Hirvonen

Translated from the original Finnish by Richard Impola.

Published by:
North Star Press of St. Cloud, Inc.
P.O. Box 451
St. Cloud, MN 56302

Printed in the United States of America by
Versa Press, Inc.
East Peoria, Il

ISBN:
0-87839-142-8

Dedication

I lovingly dedicate this book to my three grandsons Kai, George, and Julian.

Acknowledgements

My first and foremost thanks go to my husband, Phil Nast. He has been my anchor, coach, and friend throughout the years. With his encouragement and suggestions, my memories have taken shape within the confines of this book. Early in our marriage, he gave me the confidence and courage to begin to write. He understood that my passion for reading reflects that rarely were books available during my childhood.

Also, my deep appreciation goes to Dr. Richard Impola for his encouragement and for his outstanding translation of my stories, which captures the esssence of my feelings. Without him, this book would never have come to fruition.

A special thanks to my daughter, Elisa, whose artistic talents added another dimension to my stories.

A most valued asset was my "big brother," Veikko, who by virtue of his excellent memory and keen sense of humor recalled to my mind experiences that had long ago been relegated to my Finnish past. Veikko and his dear wife, Sirkka, have been my steadfast supporters throughout my life.

Table of Contents

Chapter One

Songs My Mother Taught Me

"The memories of happy moments shine through tears."

I feel the truth of this old saying most deeply on Mother's Day when, on the wings of thought, I go back again to my distant childhood and to mother. I lost her early so, sadly, my memories of her are limited. But for that reason, as the years flow by each one becomes more precious.

Mother loved flowers, songs, and strong coffee with a pinch of salt. She had a lilting laugh, and when she laughed deep dimples appeared in her cheeks. By nature, she was free and outspoken. Her relatively short earthly journey was not always an easy one. Our home was poor and it was often hard for us to get by. Yet in spite of our modest circumstances, we had riches that far surpassed what we lacked in material possessions. Mother had a bright outlook on life and was able to spread joy and beauty around her. She taught her children to enjoy simple things, to honor God, and to respect their fellow man. Never do to others what you would not have done to you, she often impressed on us. She liked to read romantic tales and demanded that we speak

1

proper literary language, while she drawled a broad *Pohjanmaa* dialect. In my brightest memories, I always see Mother and flowers. I believe that in fussing with flowers, she satisfied her longing for beauty and forgot her cares.

Then she would sing. I often stopped to listen, devoutly following the story told by the lyrics. I pitied the poor wanderer who did not dare pick the roses from the valley; I loved Black Sarah when in her joy she sang of Heaven, " . . . where there is no danger of dying, tears, not even night. . . . " I knew what the Negro girl looked like. Her picture was on the wrapper of licorice candy.

I thought long and hard about the "roses of sin" so that I would not make a mistake and pick them. The fear of going to Hell was one of a child's greatest worries in those days.

> Hear me now, where does your journey end?
> Do you know the path you go along?
> I ask your now to tell me as your friend,
> The way you've chosen- is it right or wrong?
> Roses of sin you plucked with eager hand.
> Drink deep the toasts to joy as you must needs,
> but you forget that you one day will stand
> before the Lord to answer for your deeds.

I guessed the "toasts to joy" to be the bottle from which my father sometimes took a swallow with his friends. I liked the mournful love songs better because I didn't have to ponder over their meaning. They were all about sorrow and pain, but that's part of love. Mother would sing soft and dreamily.

> No joy of life can I offer,
> no roses can I give.
> Dark foster-child of suffering,
> with grief alone I live.

2

Mother must have charmed her flowers too with her song. The windowsills of our home were full of flower pots. I remember the begonias, geraniums, and fuchsia. Passers-by often stopped to admire our windows which were radiant with color reflected from her flowers. The view was especially enchanting on a gray overcast day when the various hues appeared to capture the inner beauty of Mother. I remember when Mother was ill and Father invited the Church Provost to our home. The stern looking, big-bellied shepherd of souls looked around thoughtfully and said, "It must be difficult to die and leave here where there are such pretty flowers." I suppose it is difficult at times to express your feelings.

During the summer, the yard, except for the potato patch, became a multicolored riot of flowers. Mother had planted a row of white birches along the road, and a white rosebush flourished beside the steps. Late into the evening, Mother would labor at her favorite task.

Mother's longing for beauty was not limited to flowers alone. She also tried to mold her sturdy, round-cheeked girl into a beauty. There usually wasn't enough money to buy fabric, but a new smock would be finagled from a torn and worn-out one of Mother's, turned inside out. Then when my spiky straight mop of hair had been prettily curled, she would look admiringly at her duckling and say, "Don't I have a pretty girl."

I would climb onto a chair before the bureau and check myself in the mirror to confirm that it was so. Usually I found that I had to agree with her. But Mother could be severe too, if need be. A flexible birch switch hung over the door was our reminder to obey commands. I was spared it more than my two lively brothers, whose misdeeds I dutifully reported to my

3

mother. As payment, I received a deserved licking from my beloved brothers when Mother wasn't looking.

The spring I turned ten, our lives changed. My mother fell ill then and became bed-ridden. Incurable consumptives had to remain at home because they were no longer admitted to hospitals. Regardless, my mother would not have permitted them to separate her from her family. My eighteen-year-old brother was in the army serving at the front, in the war against the Russian invaders. My grandparents came to get my younger brother and took him to stay with them. In addition to working for a living, my father patiently took care of my invalid mother and the house. Grandmother often came to help us.

To the best of my ability, I, too, did chores. Mother never complained about her lot, but her concern for her children, who would be left motherless, ate at her heart. "How will the little girl manage in this hard world?" I could hear Mother's voice from behind the door as she poured out her grief to her friend Liisa. Liisa would mumble something about the Almighty's guidance and join in the sobbing.

Aunt Liisa was a warmhearted and an understanding woman. In spite of the pressures on her as the mistress of a large house, she found time to stop in often at our cottage. While waiting for Aunt Liisa, I would sweep the floor carefully, shake the rag rugs outside, and see to it that the table was cleared of dishes. Aunti would look around approvingly as soon as she arrived and declare, "Everything is really neat here as it always is." Patting my head she would say in a kindly manner, "You're a good girl." That noble soul did not realize how much that praise warmed a troubled child's heart. Years later, I had the joy of meeting and thanking this good fairy of my childhood. "I didn't do a thing," the old lady said surprised to hear such deep appreciation for the kindnesses that she had shown. For a moment she was lost in memory, and then she went quietly on as if she were talking to herself, "I just felt so sorry for that little girl."

Our yard was bare and desolate that spring. Black stalks protruding from the overgrown flower beds were a bleak reminder of the previous year's moment of glory. On the way home form school, I picked wild rosemary for Mother. When the ants were caught in the sticky bunch of flowers, Father threw them out the window. I don't remember if I especially liked rosemary or if no other flowers were available.

Sometimes Mother asked me to sing for her from an old hymnal. That I did gladly. I had inherited my mother's cheerful disposition and her love of flowers, but, to my sorrow, I had not inherited her lovely singing voice. Perhaps the words of the hymns brought her consolation, but that can hardly be said for my piercing, tuneless voice. I suspect, at times my singing drove my father from the house and into the woodshed, but the songs came from my heart and brought great solace to my mother. I also read to Mother from the Bible and did little things that she asked me to do. Often I felt her large pain-ridden eyes following my movements. The meaning of that gaze I understood only years later when I was rearing my own children.

The same spring brought a young fiery-souled pentecostal minister to our community. He held his services in the largest house in the village. His flock gathered to hear this charismatic speaker. In a fine voice, accompanying himself on the guitar, this man sang himself straight into the hearts of the young girls. Weeping, repenting their sins, many promised to leave the world's vanities and tread the narrow path. However, the girls forgot their promises once the handsome preacher had left the community. Children liked Jaakko-seta, as we were allowed to call him, because he always talked and sang to us. He often came to see Mother. I would offer him *ersatz* coffee. Because of shortages due to the war, we could not buy regular coffee. Each family made its own from its special recipe. Ours consisted of roasted barley and dandelion roots with a bit of chicory to add color and bit of "flavor." Jaakko-seta always politely declined my coffee. I was a little hurt by his refusal but I consoled myself with the thought that my mother didn't like it either. She longed for real coffee but she realized that it was no longer available anywhere in Finland.

Although Jaakko-seta did not care for my substitute coffee, I was delighted with his visits because I knew that they gave spiritual comfort to the invalid. I listened as he spoke in his gentle voice of Heaven and assured her that God does not abandon motherless children. I can still hear the man's melodious voice as he sang at my mother's bedside.

> Give all of yourself His sacrifice to be
> then greatly will you joy in His company.
> The Blood of the Lamb your soul will purify.
> See where spread before you
> the lands of brightness lie.
> Hurry now, hurry now, haste to Jesus stay
> Hurry now ere night o'ertake you on your way.

I believe that through the merit of this sympathetic preacher, my mother's soul found rest. I sensed it in the fact that she no longer cried. Her eyes were bright and steady when she trustingly assured us and her friend that God would take care of things. When on a lovely midsummer night Mother left for her long-awaited heavenly home, I remember feeling grateful that she no longer had to suffer. I was sure that Mother was again healthy and happy and that she could see us too, although we could not see her. It eased my missing her.

I know that Mother is happily bustling around in her Heavenly garden among her begonias, fuchsia, and geraniums. A curly headed cherub is bringing her coffee. It is black, and strong, and has a pinch of salt in it.

Thank you, Mother, for your songs.

Chapter Two

We Are All Children of the Earth

Russians were not human. They were huge beasts with long arms, filthy hair, crooked teeth, and foul breath. They raped women and killed little children. This was my Grandmother's description of the Russians, our feared enemy.

The winter of 1943 was bitterly cold even for Finland. My country had been at war with Russia for almost three years, and times were hard. Food and other supplies were difficult to obtain. People were fearful that the Russians might invade our village, and they worried about their loved ones fighting at the front. Children went to school in hand-me-down clothing. Our winter shoes had leather tops with wooden soles, while in the summer the tops were made of paper. I had a yellow-and-brown Sunday dress woven from paper. It stood up pretty well provided that I didn't get caught in the rain too often. Washing it was out of the question, so I tried to keep it clean.

At school, during recess, we played war games, pelting each other with snowballs while shouting, "Ruki veer!" which meant "hands up" in Russian. My classmates all had one thing in common—a hatred and fear of the enemy. Russians were ruthless barbarians and could not be trusted—these ideas had been implanted in our minds at a very early age.

Great excitement and concern erupted when we heard that a camp for Russian prisoners had been built in a forest just a few kilometers from the village.

At first people were terrified lest prisoners escape and ravage our village. But as time went by and nothing happened, we relaxed. Curiosity gradually overcame fear. Later, some of the more adventurous villagers went to visit the camp. They brought back little trinkets the prisoners had made from bits of light metal. These intricately fashioned bracelets and rings had been exchanged by the prisoners for food.

My schoolmate and I were fascinated by the beautiful jewelry some of the older girls brought from the camp. We wanted some for ourselves. Even more, we wanted to meet a real live Russian and see for ourselves what they looked like. When we asked the girls who had visited the camp, they just smiled condescendingly and called us stupid. In my mind, I imagined the prisoners looking like the mad monk Rasputin, whose picture I had once seen in a book.

My friend and I decided that we had to find out for ourselves whether or not the Russians were human. We made plans not to eat our school lunch that day and to set off the next morning with both days' lunches in our packs.

As meager as our sandwiches were, we knew that they would be good enough to trade for a pretty bracelet. The other girls said that the prisoners seemed to be hungry. Food was extremely scarce during the war, and even though the Finnish authorities treated their prisoners of war humanely, the rations allocated to them were much less than those civilians managed to acquire.

The next morning, instead of going to school, I met my friend on a trail behind her house. We skied through the woods to an old logging road, which we knew would lead us to the prison camp. It was a clear, crisp morning. The fresh snow seemed to sing under our skis as we glided gaily through the frosty woods. The sun was already rising, lighting our trail, but it had no mitigating effect against the biting cold. During the short winter days, the sun only had time to rise just above the treetops, where it seemed to linger just a little while to survey the frozen landscape and then quickly retreat to its warm place of refuge.

As we stopped on the crest of a hill to rest and listen to the sound of the tall pines whispering in the gentle breeze, a sudden gust of wind coursed through the snow-laden trees, loosening a white cloud, which drifted slowly toward the earth, creating a silvery veil over the landscape. The golden rays of the sun reflecting off the fine particles of snow projected a magnificent, brilliant star which appeared to fill the universe. The image lasted only an instant, but my friend and I stood there for some time overpowered by the grandeur of what we had just witnessed. In silence we proceeded.

After skiing for what seemed like hours, we came to a clearing. In its center we could see a row of low wooden buildings. Drawing closer, we realized that the area was surrounded by a high, barbed-wire fence.

Uniformed guards with rifles on their shoulders patrolled outside the fence. I recognized some people from my village talking to the guards and watching the prisoners. The scene reminded me of a zoo I had once visited, except that people stood behind the fence instead of animals. Ragged-looking men were huddled over small fires while others walked back and forth in an effort to keep warm. The men wore long, tattered brown coats and peaked hats with a red star on the front. They appeared dirty and disheveled but nothing like the monsters I had imagined. Actually, I thought, they were pitiful, miserable human beings.

In many ways the gaunt faces reminded me of the tired and cold Finnish soldiers who had passed through our village a few days before on their way from the front. I had run after them, anxiously asking if they knew of my brother.

"How should I know?" snarled a thin, bearded man, while others plodded staring straight ahead but seemingly not seeing anything.

As we removed our skis, my friend saw a handsome guard who often visited our village. She left quickly, shouting, "I'll see you later!" I took my lunch from my rucksack and, with some apprehension, slowly approached the fence. I stood there looking at the prisoners' haggard faces, when suddenly I realized that some of them were as young as my brother. Like him, they had a faint suggestion of a beard on their drawn faces, while others with weatherbeaten faces appeared old enough to be my father.

Regardless of age, a look of hopelessness and despair reflected from their dull, sunken eyes. As I moved slowly along the fence, I noticed a man holding up a faded photograph of a woman and child. It was as if he were trying to make some sort of contact with those of us on the other side of the wire. Others were displaying their trade goods in hope of getting food in exchange.

Suddenly I became aware of a tall, emaciated man with hollow cheeks and dark, sad eyes staring at me. More accurately, he stared at the small package I held in my hands. He did not appear to have anything to offer me in exchange. I stood there trying to decide whether or not I could trust this Russian to give me something in return for my food. On a sudden impulse, I thrust my offering toward him. Instantly a bony hand darted out between the wires and snatched the package from me. The man clutched his prize to his chest, mumbled something, and disappeared behind a building.

For a moment, I was angry and disappointed. I felt that my lunch had been stolen because I had not received anything in return. But gradually my feelings of betrayal subsided, and I went to find my friend. Excitedly, she told me about her conversation with the cute guard and showed me the pretty bracelet that she received for her lunch. Fearful that she would make fun of me, I lied and told her I had eaten my sandwiches.

In contrast to the morning's carefree journey, our return trip was somber. An anticipated reprimand from my angry stepmother added to the feelings of gloom I was already experiencing. The winter day was ending, and the shadows in the quiet forest cast ominous shapes over the darkening trail.

Shivers running down my spine only partly were caused by the bone-chilling cold penetrating my threadbare jacket. The sound of snow crunching under my heavy wooden skis muted my friend's chatter as she skied slowly behind me. She droned on about her visit with the guard, while my thoughts dwelled on the men on the other side of the wire. The image of the tall Russian prisoner with the sad eyes refused to leave me. I thought about my brother and wondered if he shivered in a snowy forest as cold and hungry as the man I had just seen. Perhaps somewhere in Russia the man had loved ones as worried about him as I was about my brother. I slowly realized that the feared enemy wasn't much different from us.

Years later, while studying in America, I read a poem by Stephen Vincent Benét and my childhood experience flashed into my mind. I relived that bitter cold day so long ago in my native Finland when I first began to understand that we're all children of the earth.

Grant us brotherhood,
not only this day,
but for all our years—
a brotherhood not of words
but of acts and deeds.
We are all of us Children of earth
grant us that simple knowledge.
If our brothers are oppressed,
then we are oppressed.
If they hunger, we hunger.
If their freedom is taken away,
our freedom is not secure.
—Stephen Vincent Benét

E. HIRVONEN

Chapter Three

Esko's Christmas

There is really no bad human being.
There are only the more or less weak.
There is good in every heart,
though at times it may not shine through.
For a smile is halfway to goodness,
and the wicked cannot weep.
—Eino Leino

Christmas Eve, 1942. Though only early after-noon, the sun had already dropped to the treetops as if fleeing the intensifying cold. The December day was short, a scant interval between morn and evening, and the yard still lay buried in the previous night's snowfall. Esko waded through the snow on his way to the sauna with a load of birch logs in his arms. That morning the lady of the house had said they would take a sauna bath early.

Heating the large smoke-sauna was one of Esko's many chores, one he was glad to do. It was nice to rest a bit in the heat from the fire pit and look at the cheerfully crackling birch logs. If he crouched down nearly to the floor, the smoke pouring from the *kiuas* did not sting his eyes or get into his nose. But he did not dare stay long; he still had many things to do. He

17

had to shovel the snow from the paths, carry wood into the house, feed the horses, and do whatever else the lady and others instructed him to do. Sometimes the burden of work seemed overwhelming to the slightly built eleven-year old, but it did no good to complain. On Esko's arrival at the Ruokola farm, the old master of the farm next door had advised him: "Remember that a *huutolaispoika* is always wrong. Never argue. Just do as you're told."

Worst of all was the homesickness. Whenever his thoughts strayed to his home cottage, to Father and Mother, to his sisters and brothers, a lump rose in his throat and tears welled into his eyes. He remembered his little brother's tearful voice, "Esko, Esko, don't leave me." The four-year old could not understand why he had been left in a strange home to be cared for by strangers.

Early in the spring, when Mother had wound up in the hospital, the town had assigned the four children of the family to different homes in the parish. Father had been taken to the hospital earlier. He had a cancer, Esko's older sister had said.

The Ruokola farm, to which Esko was taken, was one of the wealthiest in the community. It was run by the youngest son of the widowed lady of the house. There were also two grown sisters in the family, and that summer an old *mummo* evacuted from Karelia had come there to live. A number of evacuees who had lost their homes were lodged in the larger houses of the community.

A *huutolaispoika* was a boy auctioned off to the household which would feed, house, and clothe him at the lowest cost to the local government. He often became an unpaid hired hand for the household.

Mummo ordinarily means grandmother, but the word was often applied to an old woman, whether or not she was one's grandmother.

With the war going on at the time, all the men fit for service were at the front. Everyone in the community wondered why the young master of Ruokola was not there, for it was the duty of every citizen to defend his country. The wonder and conjectures of his neighbors did not seem to bother the man; he ran the farm with an iron hand. With the exception of occasional temporary help, the work was done by the people who lived there. Mummo Anna, who was no longer able to do outside work, often helped the mistress of the house with indoor chores. This kindly old Karelian *mummo*, who had experienced such hardships, was very friendly to Esko. She would sometimes call the boy into her room and show him photos of her long-lost family and her home cottage, now on the other side of the border. She had little else to show in her room, only a few trifles she had been able to take with her when she had been forced to flee her home. Once she took a small package tied with a blue ribbon from a drawer. Inside the silken paper was a pair of gray stockings with red stripes. They had been knitted by her daughter, and were a memento of the child she had lost to a contagious disease, Mummo told him sadly.

One snowy day, Esko had confided his great dream to Mummo Anna, his dream of getting skis of his own. She had smiled pityingly at him: "What will you do with skis, lad? You have no time for skiing." Esko knew that, and he also knew that he would get no skis until he himself could earn them. That fall Esko had succeeded in picking enough mountain-ash berries to earn money for new boots. Sundays and evenings, whenever he had time off from work, he climbed with the help of a ladder into a neighbor's mountain-ash trees. His master had given him permission. The Ruokola mountain-ash berries would be saved for the lambs, the lady of the house had declared sternly. Different kinds of jams were made from the berries, as was a powder that, when mixed with water, served as a milk substitute. The allotment of milk issued on ration cards was not enough even for the children. The mountain-ash trees in the community were picked so clean there were hardly any berries left for the birds.

The work on the farm was heavy, but Esko did his best to carry out his tasks. The most difficult thing for the slender, inexperienced boy was to manage the horses. He struggled with them often and was likely to get an angry kick from his impatient master in the process.

School was the only bright spot in Esko's wretched life. The most miserable days were those when the pressure of work kept him from school completely. In the fall, during potato-digging time, he was absent for so many days that the teacher came to the house to demand his return. In spite of his absences, the bright and eager-to-learn boy was the best pupil in his grade. Esko awoke at five in the morning to feed the horses and carry fodder to the cows. For Esko, a day in school was a pleasant day of rest.

Once he got to see his father in the hospital. For a long time thereafter tears came to his eyes when he recalled how thin and shrunken his father had become. When Esko told him about the school and his new boots, his father smiled approvingly—for the moment he could not speak. But as Esko was preparing to go, his father said suddenly, "I'm leaving tomorrow."

Esko was frightened, fearful that his father would be taken to the large provincial hospital fifty kilometers away. Esko had neither the time nor the strength to walk that far. His father did not answer Esko's panicky questions but merely gazed at him with a remarkable brightness in his eyes. The next evening, they got the news of his father's death.

That night, while the people of the house slept, Esko stood at the dark window, his thin shoulders shaking with sobs, praying that the Heavenly Father would spare his mother and let her come home again.

A few weeks before Christmas, seven-year-old twin boys had come to the farm from Helsinki, sent there by the mistress' niece to be safe from the bombings in the city. In a farmhouse, they would also be better nourished than with their scant card rations in Helsinki. The lively scamps would often trail after Esko, following his tasks with interest. Early in the week, the boys began to wait impatiently for Santa Claus. They kept guessing how many gifts there would be in Santa's pack for each of them, and what he would have for Esko.

Esko was not interested in the boys' enthusiasm. The best Christmas present he could imagine was to spend Christmas in his own home. He and his siblings' only gift from Santa had been a *pulla*-man baked by Mother. It had had raisins for eyes and mouth, and its bulging belly had been decorated with a row of raisin buttons. He remembered how good it had tasted. Mother still had real coffee then; now coffee could not even be procured with a ration card. Esko knew that the lady of the house had a supply of black-market coffee, but he knew that none would be spared for a *huutolaispoika*. He had tasted no sugar since coming to the house, although almost a half-kilo a month came on a child's card. Esko knew exactly how much.

The pale twilight of Christmas Eve had long since changed to gloomy darkness by the time Esko finished his chores. But when he stepped into the light,

In Wartime Finland

brightly decorated living room, his weariness vanished, and he felt almost happy. It was Christmas!
Esko had never seen such a sumptuous spread on
the table. He had heard the lady of the house boasting to her niece, the twins' mother, who had arrived
the day before: "We don't have to live off ration cards,
and we won't spare expenses at Christmas." There
was ham on the table, casseroles of different kinds,
and even rice pudding. Esko received only a scant
portion of the latter on his plate, but his stomach was
already full from the other offerings on the table.

Esko almost forgot his homesickness, and the little boys' eager waiting for Santa Claus began to infect
him with their excitement too. He no longer believed
in Santa Claus, big boy that he was, and probably
had never truly believed. As far back as he could
remember, he had always known that it was Father
underneath the flaxen beard and the sheepskin coat
turned inside out.

When finally Santa Claus, with a large sack on his
back, clumped into the room and asked the custom-
ary question: "Are there good children in this house?"
even Esko answered with a shy, "Yes," from where he
stood near the stove. He guessed that the Santa was
the master of the house, who had announced earlier
that he was going to take a look at the stable. Esko
gazed curiously at the bulging sack as Santa began to
read off the names on the packages. One person after
another got a gift, some more than one, but Esko's
name was not called out. "My gift must be right at the
bottom," he thought hopefully, eyes fixed on the fast-
emptying sack. The last package was for the lady of
the house.

When Santa Claus, loudly wishing everyone a
Merry Christmas, disappeared into the cold dark
night, Mummo Anna hurried to her room. Soon she

reappeared before Esko, who was squatting in front of the stove. She put a package wrapped in silken paper into his hand, and said, striving to make her voice sound gay, "Santa did have a gift for Esko too— it must have fallen from his pack." Inside the silken wrapper were the gray stockings with red stripes, and Esko knew that the Karelian *mummo* had given her dearest treasure to a despised *huutolaispoika.*

Chapter Four

My First Love

Bittersweet memories that have lingered in the pleasant recesses of my mind gradually come to the fore as the world approaches the day of lovers, Valentine's Day.

Once again, I relive my early adolescence in Finland and remember the day when I woke to the realization that there were differences between boys and girls. Until a new boy, Willy, came to school, I had been content to play with the girls in my class, but, when he arrived, my world changed forever.

Willy sat in front of me in class, and I fell in love with the back of his head. It was the cutest head that I had ever seen, small and round. The pink scalp-shining through his closely cropped blond hair looked like the inner tube of my old bicycle. When he turned his head sideways and smiled, a dimple appeared on his fat little cheek. His long white eyelashes and upturned nose reminded me of an adorable piglet that I had seen in Heglund's barn. Willy never paid the slightest attention to me, but I was satisfied to admire him from afar. I hoped that someday he might kick me under the desk or turn around and pull my pigtails. My wish finally came true.

Later that winter, Willy playfully pushed me into a snow bank and with a dimpled grin kicked snow in my face. My heart leapt for joy. He cared! Even though Willy studiously ignored me, I knew that he liked me. He was too shy to show it in front of others. The day came when an opportunity presented itself for me to find out the depth of his affection for me. At recess, all students except a monitor were ordered outside to the playground. The monitor had to open the windows to air the room, tend the fire, and clean the blackboard. As fate would have it, my monitor-duty fell on a day when the teacher had told Willy to finish his assignment during recess. I was overjoyed. At last I would be alone with my love.

As I was performing my duties, I cast furtive glances in his direction hoping he would acknowledge my presence. That was not to be. Head bowed, he kept on working furiously. I became more determined to get his attention. I wanted him to admire my nascent girlish charms and to give some sign of his true feelings. My mind raced and my heart pounded. The recall bell would soon ring. It was now or never.

I had been walking towards the front of the room a book in my hand intending to return it to my desk. The book had a pretty cover that showed children playing in a sunny flower-covered meadow. It's title was printed in golden letters, *A Child's Golden World*. I looked at Willy again with adoration tainted by frustration. On sudden impulse, I struck him on the head with the book with more passion than I had intended. The sound of the impact resembled that of the bass drum in our local village band. My first reaction was one of delight because I had finally gotten his attention. But as I watched his pink face turn to a dark red it occurred to me that I might have hurt him.

I watched in amazement as his color changed. It started at his neck, slowly spreading upwards and gradually becoming a darker shade of red as it moved to his head, which began to resemble a bright red beach ball covered with white fuzz. By then, he was emitting the first bellow that sounded like a wounded bull. At that moment, I decided that perhaps it was time for me to join my friends outside. I was running rapidly towards the door when I heard him getting to his feet. I cleared the four steps in a frantic leap. The sound of his thundering steps close behind gave wings to my feet as I sought sanctuary in the girl's outhouse. The privy was a place where he could not go and besides I could latch the door and wait until he calmed. Willy's legs were short but he could run quickly. When I was almost halfway to my place of refuge, I felt a sharp blow on my back which sent me hurling face down into the snow. Willy used me for a punching bag, hitting me with all of the force that he could muster while he cursed and called me horrible names. I was saved further punishment when, to my great relief, the recall bell sounded. Despite my sore body, I did not mind the beating too much. I loved the guy.

Chapter Five

The Hired Boy's Hill

Toward the end of the 1930s, the life of a cottager in the remote areas of Bothnia was not an easy one. Work was scarce and wages were low. There were no child-support payments or other social aid for the hard pressed; people had to manage on their own.

Thus, even the children, as soon as they could make it over the threshold, had to go out and earn money to supplement the family's small income. Many summers my oldest brother, Pauli, tended the cattle on an estate. A herd-boy did not earn much, but in addition to his wages, a hard-working lad could sometimes add a little to the food supply.

Like other boys, Pauli always had a slingshot dangling from his back pocket. Gangs of boys often gathered in the evening to compete with these self-made weapons. Pauli was their uncontested master in the noble art of target shooting.

During the long and monotonous days of wandering after the cattle, there was plenty of time for practice, and the boy became so adept that he could instantaneously knock out a rabbit loping along the edge of the field or a heath grouse hiding in a thicket. The family often had a delicious roast when the hunter returned from his herding.

Then came the spring when Pauli finished public school. Father announced that the boy was getting too old to be a herd-boy. After all, Pauli would be fourteen in a few months, of age to be a hired hand. His wages would be a little higher. Upon graduation from public school, the teacher recommended sending the intelligent and eager-to-learn boy on for further schooling. It was Pauli's dream as well, but he knew that Father's income could not be stretched that far, since it was barely enough to feed the family.

Resigned to his fate, his few possessions stuffed into his pack, his slingshot in his pocket, and Father's exhortations to diligence and honesty sounding in his ears, the boy trudged off to Kivela, a farm in the next community that was known for its penny-pinching ways.

In those days, there was no modern farm machinery to make work easier; a horse served as a tractor and the workers needed strong backs to keep the farm going.

Potatoes, skim milk, and half-rancid herring were the main menu except in the morning, when the work force got a dish of water-gruel or thin oatmeal porridge. To wash it down, the woman of the house poured out a cup of bitter coffee from a blackened copper pot. The owner's family had emptied the original contents of the pot earlier, but they added water and a bit of chicory for flavor to the dregs as an easy way of making more coffee.

The growing boy was always hungry. To appease his growling stomach, Pauli sometimes crept into the large barn at nightfall and drew a cup of nourishing warm milk from Heluna's brimming udders. But that stopped short when the man in charge of the cattle surprised him and threatened to tell the woman of the house.

Fed up with skim milk and herring, and with homesickness gnawing at his breast, Pauli ran away. My brother Jussi and I were overjoyed at our big brother's return, but father carried on about the neglect of duty and decreed that Pauli must return. But for that evening, at least, Pauli was able to sleep on a full stomach, with Casper the cat purring under his arm. In his usual fashion, Jussi sneaked his pet past Father by stuffing it into his underpants and nobly surrendered it to his big brother.

Pauli's escape was short-lived: Landowner Antti naturally did not want to lose a hard-working, low-paid hired hand. He arrived the first thing in the morning to fetch the refugee.

We watched through the window as he turned into the yard with his bicycle and wondered how he could go straight to our door with no trouble, although he was clearly looking at the barn, which was on the other side of the path. Antti was extraordinarily cross-eyed, so that a bystander could not always tell where he was looking.

But this fact could not diminish the impression of power that emanated from his massive body. We watched with respect and a touch of fear as he paced the room in his shiny jazz-boots and elegant whipcord breeches, preaching about the irresponsibility of hired hands. Finally he turned his eyes to Pauli, at least he seemed to, and roared: "You'd better come back with me now, boy." When Father reinforced his edict, the boy's tears and objections were of no avail. He had to go.

I was only about six then, but I will always remember the tragicomic sight on the road: Antti the landlord in the lead, gravely wheeling his bicycle along, then Pauli, weeping, his head hanging low, and finally Father-Nikki, threateningly waving the rod in his hand.

At the window Jussi and I kept shouting at the top of our lungs, "Jump into the woods. Jump into the woods!" Pauli could scarcely have heard our advice. Though meant to be helpful, our shouts did no good, but it did show how great was our distress at our big brother's fate. Tears glistened in Mother's eyes, too, as she stirred the porridge pot at the hearth.

Pauli did not yet know that on that morning he was bidding a final farewell to his childhood. His heavy steps as he left his home cottage were the first stumbling steps toward manhood; his struggle in the hard world of adults had begun.

One of a hired hand's jobs was to drive manure wagons to the fields. The fields were scattered over a wide area, and often loads had to be driven many kilometers. The work was unpleasant and hard for a tender boy, but it was even more repugnant to one of the farm's horses, which Pauli was given to help him in this important business.

That fine horse's name, *Into* (Zing), was a trifle misleading, for it was an exceptionally lazy animal. As to its condition, Into had been fed better than the farm's laborers; the horse was fat, and its sides gleamed, but it did not particularly like pulling a load of manure or toil of any kind. Furthermore, it had not an ounce of respect for the young hired lad.

One autumn afternoon as Pauli was driving a load of manure to Lieru Meadow in a neighboring community, Into as usual was plodding lazily along, stopping now and then to nibble at the tufts of hay on the roadside. A blow from the reins on his broad backside

only made him lower his ears and look back contemptuously as if to say, "Are you trying to order me
around, you hired hand?"

Pauli began to worry that he would not reach his
destination before evening, and that his master
would not be pleased at the delay. When Into stopped
again at the foot of Lieru Hill, the boy had had
enough. He leaped down from the wagon, backed up
a suitable distance from the calmly nibbling horse,
and loaded his slingshot.

The pellet aimed at the thick root of his tail star-
tled Into into sudden motion. He shot off with such
speed and style that even a first-class trotter would
have looked like an old nag wading in wet concrete in
comparison. But the gallop was cut short as the
wagon toppled over when it ran into a tree.

In his wild flight, Into lost his way and galloped
across the road into a woods. The valuable load had
already dribbled out as a cover for the lingon berry
bushes. Later, thankful berry pickers named the
place "The Hired Boy's Hill." This is probably the only
monument to my brother left on the soil of the place
where he was born.

When Pauli set out to salvage the load, his master
was just on the way back from a county meeting. As
the owner of a rich farm, he had an important and
influential part to play in many community affairs. In
spite of being so busy, Antti went to the church village several times a week without a worry, knowing
that the work would be done during his absence in
accord with his strict orders.

The manure wagon, which Pauli had gotten
halfway back onto the road, went clattering down the
bank when Into loosed a resounding whinny. Ears
pricked forward, the horse stared at a figure that
could be seen at intervals through the trees. Of

course, he recognized his master riding slowly down the hill on his bicycle.

To his horror, Pauli saw the bicycle fly into the ditch as Antti left the road. Roaring like an enraged mother bear rushing to the aid of her cubs, the big-bellied Antti bounded through the brush toward the indignantly whinnying Into. "He must have been stung by a wasp," suggested Pauli helpfully, looking fearfully out from behind the wagon as his breathless master began to check the flanks of his pedigreed stallion.

Relieved that the horse had suffered no injury, Antti began to help his hired boy, swearing coarsely all the while. His fine breeches were filthy and his jazz-boots scarred by the time the manure wagon was righted and the procession was back on the road again.

"So a wasp stung him, you rotten, good-for-nothing lout!" roared Antti as he picked up from the road the slingshot that Pauli had dropped in his haste. Pauli's treasure flew in an arc through the air and landed high on the top of a spruce tree, where it hung flapping like the wings of a baby crow trying to fly. Into had no desire to stay and listen to the loud-voiced lesson directed at the hired boy and started off briskly with the lightened load toward home and the supper awaiting him in his stall.

When shortly afterwards Pauli ran away again, his master did not even try to get him back. Nor would it have been easy to find him, for the boy fled to the nearest city, lied about his age, and got a job in a sawmill.

That was the start of Pauli's varied and rocky road of life. In spite of his tender age, the boy filled a man's shoes, no matter what job he was called on to do. When loneliness sometimes forced him to turn his steps homeward, he always brought gifts to the younger children. Hard work and the difficult post-war years molded the boy into full manhood, but adversity was never able to crush his sensitivity and the incomparable sense of humor latent in his nature.

Like the Spanish explorers of the 1600s, Pauli sailed to the new world to seek his fortune years later. Not actually with the same dreams as the explorers of old, who expected to find Cibola, the seven golden cities of legend, where streets paved with gold and homes heaped with treasures were there for the taking.

Pauli arrived in America knowing that dreams are fulfilled only through hard labor. He trusted in his own abilities and was not afraid of work. In addition, he had another treasure dearer than gold in the form of a life-companion. Helpful and encouraging, the energetic Katri worked by his side. Together, one supporting the other, they overcame even the most difficult obstacles. A firm belief in a better future, a sense of responsibility, and a lasting love united this incomparable pair. They found their own Cibola.

The high point of their dreams must have come on the day when their intellectually keen boy, the son of a one-time hired hand, graduated from medical school. That hired hand had always tried to obey the instructions for living instilled in his children by Father-Nikki: "Be honest, and respect God, authority, and your fellow man."

Chapter Six

The Old Threshing Barn

Gray log threshing barns squatting by the road-side have all but vanished from modern community life in Finland. They are no longer necessary. But in my childhood most grain was threshed by hand, and then every farmyard had its threshing barn. Varying images of the legendary building are deeply engraved in my memory.

During the autumn grain harvest, smoke pouring from the doorjamb and shutters of the barn was a sign that there would soon be fresh bread. But there were still many demanding steps before grain was ready for hauling to the mill to be ground into flour.

First the sheaves were dried for a few days on the rafters of the barn by keeping a fire burning on the barn floor, and then the threshing began. It was not easy to work in the hot building, which reeked of smoke. Dust and chaff invaded eyes and nostrils, and it took a sauna to wash the soot from the blackened faces of the threshing crew.

Threshing usually began at four in the morning. The sheaves were dropped from the rafters and beaten against the wall, shaking loose the first kernels from the grain heads. Then the grain was evenly spread over the floor and the remaining kernels freed by rhythmic blows from a flail. The threshing flail was a stout stick with a flat, thick piece of wood tied to one end by a leather strap. The wood thumped the floor when the thresher skillfully wielded the stick.

After the grain was loosened, the straw was saved. It was gathered up, shaken out carefully, and carried into the straw barn.

Long rye straw was used as filler for mattresses or *patjapussit,* and the remainder was chopped up in a hand-cranked chaff-cutter. Steeped in hot water, and with flour added, this made a mash for the cows and horses. Grain left in the chaff on the floor was winnowed out with a hand-turned fanning mill, again chaff and dust filled the air, eyes, and noses.

When a farm finished with its own grain, cottagers who had no threshing barn could bring the grain grown in their fields to be threshed. There were threshing machines in the community, but the older people, especially, felt that proper bread could be gotten only from barn-dried grain. Besides, straw ground up in a threshing machine was not good for mattresses.

After threshing, when the barn stood empty, occasional uses were found for it. Sometimes dances were held there. There was a lot of room, of course, and the floor, beaten to a glossy smoothness by the threshers' flails, made an excellent "parquet." In the veiled twilight of the room, suffused with the odors of smoke and grain, there was "atmosphere."

Such dances had been held from time immemorial, but my own recollections are limited to the war years, when dances were forbidden by law. The country's leaders felt it was not right for people to enjoy themselves at home when soldiers were fighting at the front for our country's freedom. In spite of the harsh times, the young craved pleasure. Almost every girl had someone "somewhere out there." Worry about them and the country's fate gnawed at everyone.

The young folk were girls and half-grown boys, but often soldiers came on leave, and then dances were organized. They were held in threshing barns or other empty buildings, depending upon where the church village's eager-beaver policeman happened to be.

The responsibility for discipline and order fell onto the broad shoulders of Constable Lindgren, who was also called *Nisupoika*. He did his duty conscientiously. The law was not broken.

Everyone made sacrifices for the war

In spite of the war, life in our community was quiet. Bombing planes sometimes roared across the skies, but we knew that they would drop their bombs on more important targets. Gang fights between villages seldom occurred, and there was no need for *Nisupoika* to tramp through the woods in pursuit of bootleggers. The necessities of life were rationed; there was nothing available to make strong drinks.

There was little need to direct traffic: only slow-moving old horses plodded along the main road. The younger, better-conditioned ones had been expropriated for use in the war. Once a day, a ramshackle, charcoal-burning bus picked up from the roadside those who were going to the city. Sometimes *Nisupoika* would carry out a surprise search and confiscate a few kilos of butter from black-market catspaws.

Once a number of soldiers happened to come to town on leave at the same time. Word was circulated immediately that a dance was being organized at the community hall. Someone hunted up a key. There were also a "gramophone" and records there.

Earlier the community hall had been a center of lively activity. Sometimes patriotic evenings were organized, where people sang and the commander of the Civil Guard gave an impassioned speech urging everyone to do his share in the common spirit of suffering and sacrifice and in supporting our soldiers, who were redeeming our right to life and independence. On his breast a medal had been affixed in the shape of an ax, which showed that he had done his share in cutting firewood, and a light metal ring on his finger testified that he had turned in his gold ring in the collection for the Winter War. Every dutiful citizen had made this sacrifice for his country. Anyone sporting a gold ring would have been branded at least a traitor.

Once an overflow crowd had filled the community hall and its yard. It happened when Finland beat Sweden in an international "march" competition.

The march was meant to show the whole world our nation's strength and unity. Sweden had been challenged to compete. Participation was a civic duty for anyone able to walk. President Ryti announced that he would take part in the march himself. The question was not one of awards or times, but of the number of participants.

Women and children were to march ten kilometers, men twenty. I started out enthusiastically too, but at the halfway mark my wood-soled shoes had rubbed my feet to blisters. The coarse sand that got in between the straps had turned the blisters on the soles of my feet to bloody wounds.

Crying, far to the rear of the line, I struggled onward. I was no longer concerned about the future of our nation, but I was determined to get the medal for the march no matter what it cost me.

"Who on earth told you to go chasing all over the

country with your Sunday shoes on?" my grandma exclaimed, as she smeared a mixture of tar and lard on my bloody, swollen feet.

As consolation she gave me a sugar cube dipped in camphor. It was what she always took when she had a chill or a pain below her heart.

The white banner with the blue cross waved from the flagpole of the community hall. My sore feet were forgotten as, with my bronze pin on my breast, I listened proudly to the Civil Guard commander's speech.

Cheeks glowing with zeal, he praised our accomplishments and assured us that the enemy would not be able to destroy our independence or enslave our heroic people. He was able to announce that one and one-half million Finns had fulfilled their civic duty by taking part in this march.

Never had the walls of the community hall echoed more thunderously with song than at the close of the ceremony, when the people sang, "Hear our sacred oath, dear Finland, (*Kuulos pyha vala kallis Suomenmaa*)/ Ne'er will force o'erthrow thee./ With our blood we shelter Thee,/ Have no care, your son stands guard."

Soon a clandestine dance was in full swing in the community hall. The windows were covered with blackout curtains and the music was playing, when an uninvited guest pounded on the door. It was Ville Salmi from a neighboring village. Ville was a well-known brawler, whom the girls seldom accepted into their group.

The boy kept bellowing and hammering at the door, but it remained closed. Cursing and threatening to squeal on the lawbreakers, he finally went away. In no time at all, Constable Lindgren was at the door, gun in hand, shouting "Open in the name of the law." When *Nisupoika* marched in, a few panicky dancers had managed to flee through the windows. The constable wrote down the names of the rest in his book, warning them that the guilty would be punished. It remained only a threat, but the law had done its duty and order had been restored.

Dances were held more commonly in a threshing barn. There were no locks on barn doors, and older people sometimes showed up. They were the carefree types, unconcerned whether their souls might enjoy heaven's bliss. Those who had undergone a religious conversion did not stray into such sinful paths. "Dancers do not go to heaven"—everyone knew that.

It was a joyful experience for younger folks when Eemeli Korpi pumped his two-row accordion, and the girls' wooden-soled shoes clumped on the floor as the boys trolled "*Iso Iita*"—"Violet's not my girl,/ not Liisa nor Tellervo./ My girl ain't so small,/and she's not so thin and weak./ Big Ida is my girl,/ Big Ida is my girl,/ And when I'm by her side,/ I'm as happy as a lark." Sometimes Eemeli would be inspired to sing "Life in the Trenches" (*Elama juoksuhaudoissa*), in his quavery voice, and then a tear always rolled down his bearded cheek. Eemeli's only son had fallen at the start of the Winter War.

Nisupoika never strayed into those dances.

I entered a threshing barn voluntarily only when dances were held there. At other times I gave them a wide berth. There were ghosts in those barns. Everyone knew that. Noise scared the ghosts away, but they always returned, or so I believed.

In those days there were no mortuaries in rural areas, and a dead member of the family would be laid out in the threshing barn until the funeral was arranged. That might take several weeks in the winter.

A funeral was an important occasion, the last

service performed for a dear one, the last show of respect. Often a caterer was hired to prepare the food, which had to be plentiful, for guests from far away had to be entertained for several days. It was an honor to receive a black-bordered letter of invitation to a funeral.

The story is told of feuding neighbors who had not exchanged a word in years. When the head of one house died, the neighbor was not invited to the funeral. Enraged, his wife complained widely, "Let them have their old funeral; there'll be a death at our place too some day."

One ate and feasted at a funeral. Even during the war there were coffee bread, sweet cakes, and ginger-snaps made with sugar-beet syrup; there were turnip casserole, fruit compote, head cheese, and herring salad. There were probably other foods, but these have stuck in my mind. In the greater houses, a service was held after the burial, and even uninvited guests were allowed to attend.

From early on, children were taught that death was a natural happening, that there was no use in fearing it ahead of time.

"Life has been given us as a gift, and no permission will be asked when it is taken away," Grandma often said. A person in mourning was consoled by the staunch belief that if one repented her sins and was converted, death was only a moving on to the joys of heaven.

It was considered a blissful fate for a little child to be granted early passage from this vale of sin and sorrow. A precondition was for her to have had the sacrament of baptism, without which her soul wandered forever in eternal timelessness.

But, even though death was not to be feared, that didn't prevent superstition and fear from surrounding that natural end. A threshing barn where a body lay was to be avoided. Ghosts lurked. The fear would vanish if you went and touched the body, but it is doubtful if anyone dared. "I'll never go into a threshing barn alive," declared Riku's Amanda when she was asked to help thresh the grain. Many believed that unrepentant souls still wandered around the barn even after the body was laid in hallowed ground. Or that a soul might come to avenge a wrong it had suffered.

That notion began to worry me after old Mrs. Rinne died and I remembered the hurtful words I had said to her. Her discolored face, covered with warts and pustules, had always been an object of wonder to me. Perhaps it was old Satan himself who once prompted me to bawl out to the old woman as she came plodding toward me: "Scabby-face, pimply-face!" I regretted my words at once, although she only glanced sternly at me and kept on going. I decided that as a result of this, the Heavenly Father, who can see our deeds and read our thoughts, would drop a hot stone on my head. It was invariably the punishment with which kids were threatened. I often wondered why the stone had to be hot—wouldn't an ordinary piece of rock dropped from the sky have served the purpose? But "the Lord moves in mysterious ways," Grandma would always sigh.

There wasn't time for the rock to fall, for the old lady stopped at my home and told my mother what I had said.

"Let this sink in, girl—you don't call old people names," Mother enlightened me as she plied my bare bottom with a limber birch switch.

I believe that the whipping atoned for my misdeed, for I never identified old Mrs. Rinne among the ghosts I saw. And there were many of the impenitent and seekers of vengeance hovering around Makela's threshing barn that winter.

I got to see them often when I went to get milk, although Mother insisted that the ghosts were born in my own stupid head.

That fall our family's only cow, Rusina, was dry and it was my job to get the milk we needed from the Makela farm. The farm was a scant kilometer away. The road ran through a gloomy woods, and I had to pass the threshing barn on the way.

Since a threshing barn was highly susceptible to fire, it was usually located far from the other buildings. The Makela barn stood at the very edge of the fields where the woods began.

The barn posed no threat during the day, but in the dark it took on a spectral form, and white shapes hovered around its black shutters. That I knew. The most spine-chilling ghost stories would always pop into my head when I neared the barn. Old people would sometimes tell such stories at night. In the familiar security of home, they did not sound so terrifying, but on a dark woods road they became believeable and terrifying.

Alina, the masseuse, had told of hearing the thump of a flail and the sound of sheaves smacking into the wall late at night from the Makela threshing barn. Once she had heard the cry of a baby there. Mother did not believe the story. She suspected that Alina had sipped on too many toddies when she had been cupping Makela. Always on such occasions she was known to have had remarkable experiences. The alcohol, which Makela always had in good supply, he got from the church village pharmacist with a doctor's prescription written for a sick cow or horse. Diluted with water, and with a little sugar added, it was a remedy for the household's ills. The recipe had to be renewed at intervals, for the Makela's pedigreed mare, Tiltu, often suffered from colic. The doctor was happy to write the prescription it in exchange for a couple of kilos of butter.

I never did hear the thump of a flail from the threshing barn, although mysterious, frightful noises buzzed around me every evening. It was worse in stormy weather when the mournful sigh of the trees and the shrill wail of the telephone wires in the wind sounded like a choir of lost souls. And then a flock of ghosts behind a dark veil would burst into view over the threshing barn. A skeptic might claim that they were patches of clouds tearing across the sky. But I recognized the figures. I tried to go faster, but lead weights on my shoes slowed me down, and the road seemed to be gliding backwards. The milk can jounced in my hand, and the milk that splashed from under its cover ran down my legs. Babbling the Lord's prayer, I struggled onward. When, panting, I reached the yard of our home, the shapes had vanished, the choir was silent, and the world was as before.

"When will you learn to walk like a human being?" grumbled Mother, as she emptied the no longer full milk can. "You always have to gallop as if there were a fire under your tail."

It did me no good to explain. Rusina calved at Christmas time, and that ended my trips for milk.

Perhaps as a result of these experiences, in later years I became interested in Edgar Allan Poe's tales of terror. I felt a kinship with the characters. The horror that Poe so vividly communicated to his readers I had personally felt as a child on the road by the threshing barn.

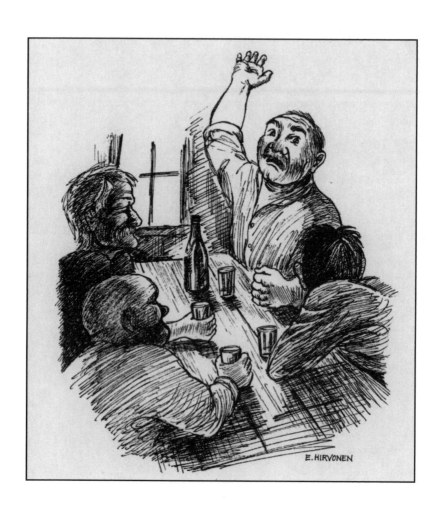

Chapter Seven

Escape

"Here comes that old gossip again," growled Father, glancing out of the window as Aliina, the masseuse, bustled up the path through the yard, almost running. To judge by her haste and the look on her face, she was on an important mission. Her round countenance, which resembled the oversized cookies in the Hanko ads, was as red as the brake light on a charcoal-burning bus, and her usual broadly smiling lips were compressed into a straight line.

Snatching up a newspaper, Father disappeared into the parlor just as Aliina stomped into the room, plopped down on a chair that was too small for her broad behind and began to mop her sweaty face with the corner of her *huivi*. I guessed that it would take a while before she could get to talking: her mouth seemed so stuffed with words that her tongue was tied.

Aliina always had interesting stories to tell. On her massaging rounds, she found out everything that happened in the whole village, if not in the whole parish. Like a sponge, she soaked in all she saw and heard, and then imparted this information to everyone, whether her listener was interested or not.

49

Aliina's news was as important to my stepmother as the morning check of her dream book or the weekly predictions of the fortune teller. I was always glad to listen to her too, but this time *The Children's Hour* was just beginning on the radio. It was the most important program of the week, and my friend Katri, who didn't have a radio at home, had come as usual to listen to it. At the same instant Uncle Markus's velvety voice said, "Hello, my little friends, hello," Aliina's word-mill rattled into motion, and my stepmother quickly turned off the radio.

"Oh Lordy, Lordy, Lordy," Aliina began with her usual invocation. Raising her voice so that it would carry into the parlor, she fired off her news, "A Russian has escaped from the camp!"

Newspaper in hand, Father appeared from the parlor and asked in a doubtful voice where she had received such information. Aliina, delighted at having gotten his attention, explained weightily that a soldier had told her on the road, and warned her to lock her doors. "I thought I should come and warn you," she said benevolently. Everyone knew that Aliina could never have gone straight home with such news.

The previous summer the camp for Russian prisoners of war had been built near the village. People had become used to its presence, and the wretched looking prisoners shivering behind barbed wire did not look that dangerous, even if they were our enemies. So that when Aliina began to intone, "Oh Lordy, what can a helpless woman do if such a beast attacks her?" I suggested helpfully that she could "sit on him."

The thought of a Russian prisoner flattened like a pancake under her sturdy bulk brought on such an uncontrollable fit of laughter that I collapsed on the floor. My brilliant advice did not amuse Katri, but then she had no sense of humor. She did not even laugh when I read jokes to her from the *Reading for Everyone* paper, jokes I, myself, laughed at so much that my stomach hurt.

Aliina directed a black and piercing look at me and barked, "What are you whinnying about, you smart-alecky moon-face." Aliina knew how to annoy me. She knew how much I suffered because of my plump cheeks, which would not shrink even if I tried to suck them in and poke dimples into them with my fingers.

Father, with a half-smile on his face, pacified Aliina: "Just go home quickly now, they'll soon catch that prisoner." To my disappointment, the *Children's Hour* was over.

The next day, two guards from the camp paced the village street, stopping in houses from time to time to warn the people. They knew exactly where the prettiest girls lived, having become acquainted with them on winter nights when they skied from the camp to the village. Katri and I had often watched with envy the fun they had in the big Purola house where the group usually gathered. Those evenings brought a little bit of life and variety to the gloomy monotony of the girls' everyday existence. All the men fit for service were at the front, and there was little entertainment for the young. Because there were so many of them, the girls had to compete for the soldiers' favor, but that did not seem to spoil their fun. The handsome guards did not even look at Katri and me. In order to look older, Katri tried to curl her hair with a fireplace poker. She scorched it badly, and got a hair-pulling from her mother. Katri was my best friend and I felt really sorry for her. She was always supposed to stay at home taking care of the younger children, so I often helped her get time for both of us to escape to the village to do things that were more fun.

That's probably why Ansu, her father, would already meet me at the door when I came to greet my friend, and shout, "Get lost, you little runt!" I did suspect that I was not a favorite in the Lahtinen house. In the past, when my mother was still alive, I had been forbidden to go to Katri's home. I would carry cockroaches from there in my clothes, she told me. I did not always observe the prohibition, but after that I was careful not to lean into the side of the fireplace at their house. Lahtinen's was the only place in the village that grew cockroaches. I had often watched with interest as they darted along the wall, disappearing at times into cracks in the bricks. They were large and shiny brown. Katri, noticing my interest, trapped a cockroach with long feelers in a match box and urged me eagerly, "Hey, take it home." Afraid that it would freeze, I rocked it in my pocket on the way home. But when Mother saw the contents of the box she screamed and threw it into a snow bank. I felt a bit of pity for the fate of the cockroach, which was used to the warmth from the stove.

When the prisoner had not yet been found on the second day, Kusti Tahvo, the old America traveler, could be seen in the yard of the co-op store gathering a search party, or a posse, as they said in America. Although Kusti's left leg, hurt in a mine accident in Louisiana, was noticeably shorter than his right, he bounced around as nimbly as a jackrabbit among the assembled group and declared enthusiastically: "Let those kids who wave their good-for-nothing guns around stay put. The men are taking charge now." Kusti had an old hunting rifle for a weapon, and a powder horn hung at his waist. That was all a person needed, he affirmed.

Three sturdy menfolk reported for the hunt: Big Hemppa, Nestor Halme, and Emil, the shoemaker.

Since Kusti's tin-plate canteen, which he always carried in his breast pocket, was empty, it was decided to go first to Ojala's. In America, palavers always took place in a saloon, he enlightened the men. The hallway at Ojala's served as the village saloon, but it was seldom open. Jaakko was the best at the business of distilling liquor, but the supplies needed for it were hard to aquire in those days. But, the joyous word had been heard that Jaakko had just finished a batch. This time not even *Nisupoika*, the zealous policeman of the village, had got wind of the matter, even though he was always snooping into Jaakko's activities. There was a liquor store in the city where one got a certain ration per month on his card, but since there was a shortage of food, city-dwellers often exchanged their liquor ration for butter and eggs. Thus Kusti did not have to scrimp along on the ration card allowance; he could help out his fellow man and fill his canteen as a reward.

When the palaver began in the hallway, Kusti demanded free refreshments for the posse. Hilma, Jaakko's wife, later explained. "We are working for the common good," Kusti had intoned, waving his hands. "Ready to save the women and children from the clutches of the enemy." That did not soften Hilma; money was needed to care for her flock of kids. But as the night went on, Kusti stopped grousing and his purse strings loosened as Jaakko's supply decreased. At the same time, he laid out plans for where they should begin their search, but in between, in his usual way, he got interested in telling about his adventures in the West. His oft-repeated reminiscences of the exotic black girls of Louisiana never lost their luster. Although the other men had only seen them in pictures, Kusti's detailed descriptions of the charms of the dark beauties always cast a spell over his listeners.

After midnight the posse had been seen, or rather heard, stumbling along the village street, whooping at the top of their lungs: "We'll do okay, we'll do okay,/ we've still got five marks left to pay/ for a bottle of liquor./ Tomorrow is another day,/ so let's live it up while we still may."

When the escapee was still missing on the third day, in spite of an intensive search, the residents began to mutter about the ineffectiveness of the searchers. Even Aliina had not dared to leave her house in order to replenish her store of information for two whole days. The villagers were convinced that the prisoner would not try to get to the border. "The Ivans would put a bullet through his skull even if he made it across," Ansu Lahtinen predicted gloomily.

That night even I was able to follow the exciting hunt when I stopped at the Nikula's on my way home. Scary tales of the hidden escapee had affected me too, and in spite of the bright summer evening the last short stretch of woods on the way home seemed threatening. Nikula's house, which was a little outside the village, seemed a nice place to stop. I had often spent nights in the bed by the door, asleep behind the broad back of Sanna, the mistress of the house. Her daughter, Mirja, slept in the bedroom. There was no one else in the house.

I admired Mirja extraordinarily. She shared with me her correspondence romances. During the war, civilians were urged to remember the soldiers fighting on the front with letters and packages. Mirja took the exhortation to heart. Almost daily she sent by army mail a letter to "out there somewhere." A letter addressed to an unknown soldier soon resulted in a lively correspondence. I thought that Mirja was able to write romantically. Actually she was helped a little by a book called *A Guide to Correspondence* that she ordered from Helsinki. She often borrowed profound thoughts from the book. Sometimes photographs would be exchanged. For that purpose Mirja would go to the best photo studio in the city to have her picture taken. In it she looked almost like a film star. Her hair fell in artful waves and I could hardly recognize Mirja's own potato-shaped nose in the retouched picture. Once a corporal came to meet Mirja on his leave, but no serious romance developed from it. Mirja guessed that he might have come just to see the size of the farm.

Later that evening a tall, handsome soldier came into the house and asked for a bed for the night. Gravely he explained that the prisoner was believed to be hiding nearby, and that by checking the surroundings from the house, he could make sure. No further explanation was necessary; Mirja and I rushed into the bedroom to make up a bed for the important visitor. "He has a sergeant's rank," whispered Mirja, rigid with admiration as she slid the photo of her last pen pal into a desk drawer.

The sergeant asked Sanna for a loaf of bread, which he set on a grindstone bench near the fence. "If it disappears during the night, we'll know that the prisoner is holed up near here," he explained.

"The mosquitoes will shit on the bread," fussed Sanna, trying to cover the loaf with a newspaper. The sergeant removed the paper, saying that that would not spoil the bread. "Who will pay for it, the Russian?" Sanna insisted, annoyed.

"The state will pay," the sergeant consoled her.

"Yeah, we'll see when the war is over," shrilled Sanna, and stormed into the house, her skirts flying.

I waited impatiently in the house for the war hero, who had sat down next to Mirja on the storehouse steps, to come back in and tell exciting stories about battles at the front. My disappointment was great when the pair finally returned and immediately disappeared into Mirja's bedroom. Late at night I stared bleary-eyed out of the window waiting for someone to come and get the bread. I did not have to be afraid; I knew that my protector was in the bedroom.

In the morning the bread was still there when the sergeant, after a well-earned rest, returned to his demanding duties. That same evening a hungry, mosquito-bitten escaped prisoner walked back into the camp. For many days, people spoke of the danger they may have experienced. But, gradually peace returned to the village.

Chapter Eight

Tales Told by a Western Logger

Most Finns know *Lannen lokari* (Western Logger), the Hiski Salomaa song about the Lothario of the timberlands who wooed the women from Maine to Honolulu. The *Lannen lokari* of this tale may not be the quite as dashing as the one in the Salomaa song, but I found him more amusing and true to life.

> *Haikatu tiiraa nelikatu taa*
> *Sipikati sipikati harkitsoo,*
> *taara taara kumppurei*
> *Haikatu tiiraa nelikatu*
> *taa systeri tiira valtimo*
> *Taara taara kumppurei,*
> *taara taara kumppurei.*

Kusti Tahvo would sing this in his quavering, old-man's voice as he beat time with the turned-up toe of his Lapland boot. I had heard the song so many times that its extraordinary words were permanently embedded in my mind. It was *inklis*, Kusti declared. He had been to America, he knew the language, and he told interesting stories that I never tired of hearing. Exotic-sounding names like *Lusiaana, Misikaani, Nyyjorkki* cast a fairy glow over the world of my imagination, while providing me with scraps of knowledge about a great land that a child in this distant region of the world could have only dim notions.

As was usual in that time and place, Kusti and his buddy Janne departed for America at the start of the century. Their goal was to earn dollars to buy a farm. Kusti was still a bachelor, but Janne left a family behind, vowing to his wife that he would return as soon as he had a pile of those dollars. In a few years Kusti returned with the report that Janne, in addition to the dollars, had acquired a new family. That was the last ever heard of him. People started calling Janne's wife "an American widow." Soon after he returned, Kusti bought a farm and married lusty Liisa Halme. Together they tilled the soil and raised a pack of kids. When the oldest boy took over the farm, Kusti no longer did any appreciable share of the farm work but tramped the woods with a shotgun on his back and a powder horn at his belt. His breast pocket often bulged with a small metal canteen, medicine for his rheumatism, he explained.

Often when a group of men gathered at our house to taste Father's highly praised homemade rye elixir, Kusti got to telling stories of his western adventures. Although in appearance he was a small, wizened runt of a man, when he went back in memory to his youth, waving his hands and bounding up on his one sound leg, intoning how men collapsed like hay in a hailstorm, and how the saloon emptied of rowdies when a Finnish lad was setting things to right, one could believe that in his prime, Kusti had been a tough man. He boasted of once having knocked a six-foot cowboy to his knees for uttering unseemly words in the presence of ladies. He himself had always been a gentleman, as one ought to be. At least in America, he said pedagogically.

A mine accident in Louisiana crippled Kusti for life and cut short his American pilgrimage. As a result, one of his legs was shorter than the other, making his walk an odd sort of bobbing. It did not interfere with his working, and he moved nimbly about his tasks, but the slightest obstacle in his path brought forth a flood of profanity. Its effect was dampened, however, by his fuzzy "R's," which made his cursing sound almost funny.

One time, Kusti loosed a torrent of curses at me. It happened after he had drunk a little too much, dozed off in our rocker, and I, at my brothers' urging and advice, drew a funny picture on his bald head with a grease pencil. The older and wiser boys knew that when the identity of the artist was revealed, a stupid and uncomprehending girl would escape with a lighter punishment. The drawing did evoke general hilarity until annoyed Mistress Lissu buffed the bald head to its former glow.

The episode left enough artistic instinct sprouting in me so that I began to eye Shoemaker Emil's gleaming bald dome wistfully. Its breadth made it a much more inviting canvas than Kusti's little moonshape. It was probably to my benefit that Emil never dozed off at our house. He lacked even the limited sense of humor that Kusti had. He always lost his temper when boys chanted as they passed by him: "You can pull the bald-headed shoemaker's hair with the help of a sticking plaster. . . . "

As an experienced world traveler, Kusti enjoyed a certain prestige among the village fathers. Many of them had never journeyed beyond the mill at Ylikyla. Others had indeed crossed "the pond," but Kusti was the only one left of the few who had returned.

According to his boasting, Kusti had been quite the Don Juan in the exotic world of Southern women. The men listened to his adventures them with rapt attention.

The detailed accounts of enchanting black girls in Louisiana usually exceeded my limited understanding. The only thing I recall is the flamboyant final statement. It was always the same, an admonition usually directed at spindly Einari, the tinker, if he happened to be there. Einari was inclined to laugh at the stories. Sucking on his roll-your-own cigarette, Kusti would fix him with a condescending stare and say in a knowing voice: "Listen, old man, if you ever saw the bare bottom of a black girl by lamplight, you'd die like a louse." I remember wondering why the sight would have such tragic consequences, but since none of us had ever seen a black person even by daylight, how was one to know?

Spindly Einari was a roving tinker, and, in his years of wandering from village to village, he must have accumulated his share of experiences. He had even been to Helsinki. Thus he was not impressed by Kusti's boasting. In those days, a copper coffee pot was one of a household's most important utensils, and a periodic tinning was a part of its proper maintenance. Although the housewives complained that Einari ruined more pots than he tinned well, he was the only practitioner of the trade in the area, and pots and pans that needed repair always materialized whenever he appeared in a house. The trademark of the tall, lean tinker was his tinner's retort, which always stuck out of the knapsack on his back. But he was so pitifully emaciated that when he stood behind an iron bar, only his ears were visible. At least, that's what my father claimed.

The stories I most liked to hear from Kusti were lumberjack tales from the Michigan logging camps. Finns were often sought in the woods, Kusti recalled proudly. The timber barons even built saunas at the logging camps to lure Finns to them. The lumberjacks were real men, no *menno milksops* or mama's boys could even begin to match them, he enlightened us, glaring critically at his listeners from under his bushy eyebrows. They worked fourteen hours a day, and life was monotonous, far from human habitation for months at time. It did have its advantages, for the dollars mounted when there were no girls or saloons around, he admitted.

Kusti attached the same value to horses as to men. They were the timber barons' prized possessions, he explained. They were generally cared for well. A supply of medicines and salves was kept for them, but for a lumberjack's wound, a splash of whiskey and a wad of chewing tobacco were considered sufficient medication. Accidents seldom happened, Kusti boasted. The men were expert in the use of the crosscut saw and the two-bladed ax. Sometimes accidents occurred when loading logs, so the pay was higher for that work.

Once he showed us pictures of a load of logs the size of a house. Compared to it, the team of horses hitched to the sled seemed helplessly small. One of the men expressed a doubt that those nags could pull the load. Kusti really flared up then, declaring that not one of this place's sway-backed crowbaits could even begin to match those horses. Since Kusti had no horses at the time, he often spoke contemptuously of those owned by others. No one reproached him for it, since it was known that everything was bigger and better in America. Kusti did admit that two horses, no matter how extraordinary they might have been, could not just walk away with that giant load. They needed help. The logging road was frozen over and ruts along which the sled runners could slide easily were hacked into the thick ice. On downhill stretches, straw or hay was spread to act as a brake; otherwise the load could slide down at a terrific speed and crushed the horses under it.

I never saw the pictures again, but Kusti often recalled his days as a lumberjack, vowing that many a pine tree would have been left standing and many inhabitants of a sauna-less camp would have been smothered by lice if Finns had not been recruited to come to the rescue.

Kusti told of digging iron ore one winter—it must have been in Minnesota. During that time, he lived in a boarding house run by a Finnish woman. She could not speak English, and on one occasion Kusti had to act as her interpreter. The supply of coal for the stove had run out. There would be no money until the following week when the men were to be paid. The landlady and Kusti set off for the store. Decades later he could still remember how he said his piece. "Gimii kolia. Next viikon *perjantaina* (Friday) on peidei. Lotsa men *paleltuu* (freeze) upsteers. *Kyllas ymmarat jos antaa tahrot.*" (You do understand if you want to give us coal.)

They got the coal.

That was my first English lesson. I added a bit of gibberish to it, and won my friends' admiration for my linguistic skill. Of course that did not last long, since my vocabulary never developed beyond that point, and my friends began to doubt the authenticity of my babbling.

Kusti pried out the last of his dollars deep in a Louisiana salt mine, where he left the best years of his manhood. He received no compensation for the accident, but there was no sign of bitterness or rancor in his reminiscences. He always made it clear that his brightest memories of the years in America were of the dusky girls of Louisiana.

Years later when I heard the familiar sounding

melody, "Ta ra ra boom de ay," I remembered hearing similar verses with slightly different words, on the hearthstone of my childhood home. I compared the versions and concluded that the original could not stand comparison with the version of Kusti Tahvo.

Chapter Nine

Nikki

Don't weep my dearest darling
I'll come if God but grant.
But if I should fall in the field,
comrades will bring you my farewell.

They'll tell of my longing for you,
of my love, and the way I died;
the mound where my body lies buried
and how love led me to that grave.

Nikki's sorrowful song broke off when the accordion
gave a discordant whine. The old two-row squeeze box
groaned and complained as he tried to pump life into its
asthmatic lungs. Finally it emitted a series of notes that
were bright and clear. The player's tense face relaxed
into a kind of smile, and cautiously he stretched the old
instrument's bellows to their full extent as he essayed a
new verse. Again the plaintive, melodic song floated
through the gloom of the summer evening.

And how love of a country and people
but really my love for you
led me bravely to go into battle,
and was cause of my death in the end.

Nikki did know more cheerful songs. He had
even played at dances, but that summer when he sat

on the well cover with his accordion on his knee, the listeners who gathered around him were in no mood for empty falderal. A war was going on. Men were fighting and dying at the front. Nikki's melancholy songs released pent-up feelings, often in tears, and united the listeners. The worry and grief were shared by everyone.

The war had lasted for more than three years now, and the daily news reports on the radio, which listed the number of enemy tanks destroyed and planes shot down no longer gave us confidence of victory. Nor could we believe the assurances that "our own losses were slight." To our small community they were no longer slight. The white crosses on the heroes' graves near the church testified to that.

Nikki knew how to interpret the sorrowful songs. He understood the sorrows and fears of his listeners. He himself had seen the horrors of war, had fought as a young soldier for the freedom of his people and had been wounded. He and his newlywed wife had undergone years of suffering after the war for freedom, when bitter poverty, great unemployment, illness, and many other social problems prevailed in the country. The young couple lost their first two little ones to epidemics. After them came five more children, only two of whom survived to adulthood. Mother Selma did not get to see them grow up. Tuberculosis cut off her busy life when she was only forty. Life was severe and merciless. Nikki knew it well.

Nikki was born on a sauna bench as the fifth and last child of Kaisa, the widow of a tenant farmer, in August of 1895. His father, Juho, had died in an epidemic early that spring. The child was baptized Nikolai. It was then the custom to name boys after the reigning czar, and Nikolai II had ascended the throne of Russia the previous year. Perhaps it was hoped that the name would signify a brighter future for a people struggling with difficulties. The name probably lost favor a few years later when a namesake, Nikolai Ivanovitch Bobrikov, became governor-general of Finland.

This dictator, appointed by the czar, caused the people greater and greater suffering and tried to take from them the few rights they had. Nikki's most significant childhood memory was of the day when the hated "Poprikoffi" got the reward the people wished for him. Nine-year-old Nikki was attending an itinerant school, for public schools had not yet reached the outlying villages of Pohjanmaa. By then his three oldest brothers had gone to America. Fear of being drafted into the Russian army led many a young man to leave the land of his birth. Two of the brothers returned in time, but the oldest, Oskari, chose a new homeland.

The itinerant school was held in the large main room at Honkala. Nestori Kontio, a fiery patriot, was acting as the teacher. Tumultuous news had arrived in the village, which Nestor conveyed to his pupils as glad tidings: Bobrikov had been shot in the Senate marketplace in Helsinki. The executer of this heroic deed, Eugen Schauman, had attoned for it by immediately shooting himself, the teacher explained. He ordered the pupils to write the name, which was difficult to spell, in their notebooks. Nikki remembered helping Hakala's grown-up first-born with it Heikki could not seem to keep the letters in his burry head. Adults came to the itinerant school as well, to learn the art of reading, for they had to pass confirmation school if they meant to marry, and that was Heikki's aim. Although Nikki knew that Heikki never did learn the noble art of reading, the lad did later sit down to communion with the rest. It was said that before this occurred, Heikki's father, the master of Hakala, had been seen leading a large bull-calf to the parsonage. Gifts were acceptable to the Servant of the Lord as well.

It was the itinerant school that awakened Nikki's desire to read. Even when he was old he followed world events closely with the aid of books and newspapers.

Nikki's most outstanding character trait was his incomparable sense of humor. It did not manifest itself in the uproarious telling of jokes, but in quietly witty comments that were always perfectly suited to the situation. His occasional moods of depression were lightened by the bright and happy outlook on life of his wife, Selma. As a father, Nikki was demanding and often severe, but always responsible and honest. He had a firm faith in the guidance of the Supreme Being, although he seldom went to church. Probably a contributory cause of the latter was the big-bellied parish dean's knowledge of every parishioner's sins, whether they were sins of commission or omission. At the start of every forceful sermon he let the world know what a wretched, sinful flock he had before him. He predicted with certainty that every last one of them would wind up in Hell's fiery furnace and saw little hope of any conversion. The heaviest among Nikki's burden of sins were probably liquor and card-playing, against which the dean often warned his flock. But was the Servant of the Lord blameless himself? At any rate the story was told that when during one of his hellfire and brimstone sermons he drew a handkerchief from the pocket of his gown, a playing card came out with it. Slowly it floated down from the pulpit to land at Hevos Kaapo's feet. "Wh-what is it?" barked the dean. "The ace of spades," Kaapo announced firmly. The Servant of the Lord was not at all taken aback, but roared in a tone of reprimand: "You know your cards well enough, but do you know the word of the Lord?"

"Card-cheat," Kaapo muttered.

Cardplaying was a pastime the men practiced out in the woods during the summer, hidden away from their wives. It was not only a violation of the Sabbath, but the father of a family might lose his week's earnings there and wives certainly were against that. Nikki was a favorite at these sessions, for he often had a bottle in his breast pocket, which went the rounds from man to man. The contents were homemade and were praised as excellent. The highest accolade was given by Ansu Korpi, whom Nikki had named the "horizon painter" because of his artistic abilities. This is what Ansu said: "It is sharp on the tongue, but glows in the innards. It warms a man for a long time afterwards. It clarifies thoughts and brightens the soul." Nikki remembered this statement, and for its merit he always gave Ansu a drink if there happened to be any liquor in the house when Ansu visited.

Ansu never had any money, for he didn't care a rap about work. The Korpi family was the only one in the community that lived on community relief. In those days, many a family would suffer hunger rather than stoop to ask aid from the county. It was said of Ansu that as a baby he had been kept on the upper bench when the sauna was too hot, which had clogged his channels of thought a little bit. He had so many kids that they could be counted only when they barged out single file through the door, Nikki claimed. When he went to get the weekly load of essentials from the county office, an official asked for the current count of Ansu's family members.

Carefully, using his fingers to help, he reckoned them up: "Me and the wife, that's one; Aatu and Ville, that's two; Silvi and Hanna, that's three; Ylli and the little boy, that's four." After that, the family increased by a half.

Nikki's "joy juice" enterprise brought in a little extra income to the family, for job possibilities were very limited. Competition developed, for there were other local distillers. Quality was crucial, and public opinion rated Nikki's goods as the best. Shortages during the war, when materials were hard to acquire, stifled many a budding enterprise. Nikki's output shrank too, at times to zero. A constant annoyance was Constable Lindgren, the *Nisupoika*, a fat, bow-legged representative of officialdom, who spied on Nikki's activities, and who once learned of his hidden plant in the woods and surprised him in the very act. A trial followed, and the fist of the law sentenced the criminal to half a year in jail. A merciful judge allowed the prisoner a choice of food that would shorten his prison term: bread and water. In a month, a slimmed-down Nikki was a free man again, and his thankful customers at the "Saloon of a Thousand Delights" took up a collection to benefit his family.

The proper name of this establishment, which stood next to the bus station in the city, was Santu's Kitchen, but Nikki had given it a name he felt it better merited. What delights were served up there only the circle of customers knew. It was a den of sin, claimed the women. The Saloon of a Thousand Delights was a favorite meeting place for males going to town. Soldiers on leave often stopped off there.

Santu served whatever food was obtainable at the time, along with pilsner and coffee substitute, which anyone could spike from his bottle, if he had one. The farmers brought in food items in exchange for other products. The card ration granted by the liquor store was hardly enough to make a one-legged man stagger. It was believed that the glib-tongued Santu paid off the officials with gifts. It wasn't for nothing that Nikki dubbed him "Windmill-spinner": his words flowed as if from a mill cranked by an unseen hand.

Once when the itinerant tinker, Einari, was passing through the city on the way to our village, he, as usual, spent a pleasant day in the Saloon of a Thousand Delights. When he left the city aboard the last charcoal-burning bus of the day, he was forced to get off at the stop outside the village. There he flopped down alongside the road, and there Nikki found him early in the morning, blissfully asleep with his pack for a pillow. From it jutted a *kolvi*, the long retort used in the tinker's trade. Nikki tore the cover from a large Tyomies tobacco carton and printed a verse on it. "You tinned a lot,/ you ruined a lot,/ but in the end your *kolvi* grew cold." Nikki placed the memorial verse on the weary traveler's chest and stationed himself behind a bush to watch the course of events.

The first to stride into view was the Kivel dairymaid, Mari, who was on her way from milking in the Lieru back meadow. Mari was a large, loud-voiced woman who, as people used to say, "wasn't dealing from a full deck." I thought the expression completely misleading, for women didn't play cards. So Mari stood there on the edge of the ditch bellowing out to church-goers rushing by, "Come here, for Pete's sake, there's a dead man lying here! He's even got verses on his chest." Finally awakened by the commotion, Einari headed toward the village, dragging his pack and cursing out crazy women.

Life was not easy, but Nikki was able to color even the darkest of scenes with humor. Not having a particular trade, he supported his family with what-ever temporary work became available. Among his employers was Antti Kivela, the owner of a large farm, who was known for his miserliness. His stinginess as well as his crossed eyes often gave Nikki subjects for good-natured mockery. Once, in helping Antti build a fence, he was holding the pole that Antti was about to drive in with a sledge hammer. Looking up, he saw that Antti's cross-eyed gaze was focused directly on his own head. "Are you going to hit what you're look-ing at?" he asked nervously.

"Of course," growled Antti, raising his sledge.

Letting the post fall, Nikki cried out: "I'm getting out of here."

Nikki condemned Antti's so completely in his greed for money that no trees were left on which birds could perch when they sang. In the spring, the cuck-oo had to call lying on his back on tussocks, he com-plained. During the winters, Nikki himself often worked felling the trees, though Antti was not always satisfied with the results.

"You're wasting wood," he complained, looking at high stumps above the snow. "You have to cut right at the base," he explained.

Nikki knew that he had not always cleared the snow from around the foot of a tree to be felled as well as he should have, but he could not admit that to the owner. Instead he decided to show off his book learn-ing, and asked Antti, "Have you read Newton's law?" knowing full well that Antti's reading was restricted to Agriculture and Forestry publications. Nikki, who had studied Isaac Newton, enlightened Antti peda-gogically: "Newton says that for every action, there is and equal and opposite reaction. Thus, when a heavy tree falls off a stump, that stump springs upward." Antti never quite knew what to say.

Just as a people has a government, so too does a family, which is ruled by the master of the house. The discipline here has to be so strict, Nikki would say playfully, that when the master steps in, the wife and cat scoot out through the back window.

According to the history books, the Finnish government has fallen a number of times, and according to Nikki, that could also happen in a family, as it did at Shoemaker Emil's house. A card game was going on there. Without his wife's knowing, Matti Halli had secretly slipped over to play. His wife did not approve of cardplaying. Usually Matti lived according to his large wife's wishes. The men laughed about the woman's rule in the Halli household, and the women were a little envious. Sometimes Matti succeeded in slipping away from Hulda's possessive domination and then he would be seen on the road a little tipsy, his face, which resembled a frozen potato, beaming with happiness.

"This is Matti out here in the world,/ and though my stature may be short,/ this wretched world can never change/ my happiness to grief," he would sing. Not daring to show himself to Hulda in that state, he would take his rest on a rail fence by the roadside. Knee joints slack, arms spread wide, he would hang sprawled over the fence. "Matti is sleeping in a bow-tie knot," passers-by would say with a laugh.

The card game at Shoemaker Emil's house was in full swing when there was a knock at the door. Opening it cautiously, Emil saw Hulda there. Loudly, she inquired after her husband. "No one has seen him," Emil assured her, trying to close the door. Hulda's hefty bulk slammed into it, knocking Emil flat on the hallway floor. The floorboards boomed as Hulda strode over the man, who scrabbled away from her on his back. Before he could get up on his pegs,

Hulda had dragged her struggling better half out by the neck. The next day Nikki announced this news in the village: the government has fallen in Shoemaker Emil's house.

Probably the biggest factor in Nikki's remarriage was buttermilk. He loved that drink. It was excellent medicine, especially for a hangover. His fondness for buttermilk was noted by Hanna, a nimble little widow who lived in a little house deep in the woods. The road to it was very poor, practically impossible to negotiate during the spring and fall. "If someone dies there, the only way to get the body out is to lead it," Nikki would say. Hanna had two cows and made butter from the milk they gave. The butter she sold at a high price to black-market dealers. The buttermilk was good and thick, with many bits of butter floating in it.

Tired of solitude and of tramping the muddy road, Nikki agreed at length to the widow's urgent solicitations to move into her house. Buttermilk continued to appear on the table, even though the days of the black market were over, but a marriage based on buttermilk alone turned sour after a few years. Probably a contributing factor to the breakup was Nikki's failing health, which made him more impatient. "I'm an avid reader," he complained, "but she is satisfied to check the dream book in the morning, and her desire for knowledge is quenched by the weekly fortune-teller's prophecy."

Nikki did not marry again, but when he moved to the city, he was an enthusiastic go-between for widows seeking marriage companions. With his love of company and his sense of humor, he was an outstanding success in that endeavor, and received the thanks of many wedded couples who had found happiness through him. Nikki's eventful life ended at the age of ninety.

Nikki

Nikki had the same goodness and the same weaknesses we all harbor, but what I remember best are his positive attitude to life and his sense of humor. Nikki was my father. After all these decades I can still see him sitting on the well-cover with his accordion on his knee and hear his mournful song:

The waves of life rise high,
and through them runs my way.
I don't know the end of my journey
be it bliss or the blankness of death.

Chapter Ten

My Pet Goat Papu

I knew that I should stop him. The angel on my shoulder told me to stop the impending disaster. But it was too late. I was rolling in the grass, convulsed with hysterical laughter, unable to do anything except to anticipate what would happen next.

My pet goat, Papu, had been sweet and cuddly when small, but as he grew bigger and bigger and started to follow me to school, he developed the annoying habit of "kiddingly" butting my classmates. He didn't mean to hurt them. He only wanted to join our group, and that was the only way he knew how to play. When our teacher saw what he was doing, Papu was banished from the schoolyard forever. I suspected that my fourth-grade teacher did not like goats.

I tried very hard to break Papu of his playful but annoying pastime, but occasionally, when that irresistible urge seized him, he would succumb to temptation and revert to his old tricks. Thus it was, on this particular day, that I could see by the gleam in his eyes that Papu had located a suitable target. He suddenly stopped at the barn door. His slanted yellow eyes were directed towards my father, who was digging potatoes on the other side of the yard. Papu's intense stare was focused on my father's wide posterior as it rhythmically bounced up and down when he reached for potatoes and threw them into a basket.

It was not until Papu started to tilt his head from side to side and step back as if to measure the distance to the target that I fully realized that he was planning to give my father the goat's version of a "trip to the moon." Papu's eyes seemed to grow brighter and his eyelids closed slightly as if he were making careful calculations. Not quite satisfied, he would step forward and back, stop, then repeat the process.

He seemed to know exactly when the right distance was reached and he was ready to charge.

When I saw a diabolical grin appear on his gentle face, I knew for sure that the inevitable would happen. I could do nothing to stop the disaster that was about to occur. Papu lowered his head, pawed the ground, and with a sardonic "baaaa" hurled his body toward his unsuspecting victim. Almost immediately I heard a thud followed by a scream of rage. As I raised my head and wiped tears of laughter from my eyes, I saw my father's muddy frame rising from the ground as Papu rapidly disappeared into the woods pursued by my father's thunderous Lutheran oaths and the threat that there would be "goat meat on the table tonight." Suddenly it occurred to me that my presence was no longer needed, so I too rapidly disappeared around the side of the barn.

Elisa Hirvonen

Chapter Eleven

Glimpses into the Past

As I walked the familiar route, I could see that the co-op store was still standing alongside the gravel road. It seemed to have shrunk over the decades; I had always remembered it as larger. The corner boards were slightly awry and the paint flaking from its window frames, but a placard in the window showed that the old community store was still doing business in the usual way. The placard advertised this week's blockbusters: Poutu's Saturday sausage and Oltermann's cheese, at bargain prices. One solitary bicycle stood in the rack beside the front steps. The yard looked deserted.

Only the serenade of songbirds and the incessant buzzing of bees in the gnarled apple tree broke the silence of the spring morning. The distant honk of an automobile horn was a reminder of the outside world, of the main highway, which by-passed the town and the old co-op store. The new age of the automobile enticed customers to larger shopping centers, where one could find a more varied selection of goods and better prices.

The local store is no longer necessary except for small, indispensable purchases. During my childhood, it was the center of the community. There one could find everything needed in a household. If it wasn't there, it wasn't necessary. I remember the warm and homey smell of the store, in which one could distinguish the scents of oil paint, of leather boots, and of peppermint.

In those days old Nestor Nupponen ran the store. I took many a paper cone filled with butterscotch and peppermint candy from his hand. Sweets were then a rare delicacy. When I pried a penny loose from somewhere, I headed straight for the store.

"What kind would you like?" the storekeeper would ask courteously, tearing off a piece of wrapping paper to make the small cone.

He often had to wait before a decision was made as to size, color, and variety. Price also had to be pondered. One's choice of candy must not be rushed. Nestor was a patient man.

Once when I was about seven, I got permission to spend the day at a cousin's in the neighboring village. The night before, my mother gave me fifty cents with which to buy gifts for the visit.

I woke up early thinking of how we would play that day, and when the clock on the wall struck six, I crept out into the summer morning. I decided that I should get right down to business. The birds were already singing at full volume, and near the doorway, Casper was gnawing at his breakfast, growling loudly. Only the tail of the mouse he had caught was still visible.

Half running, clutching the coin in my hand, I sped toward the co-op store. I knew that it didn't open until nine, but I also knew that Nestor's lodging was in the same building as the store. Once I had gone in by way of it on an errand for my mother after store hours, and he hadn't seemed to mind.

This time I had to hammer at the door for a long time before Nestor's tousled head appeared in the doorway. Rubbing his eyes, one hand holding up his long johns, a frightened look on his face, the poor man kept repeating:

"What's wrong? What's wrong?"

"I need fifty cents worth of candy, thank you," I explained breathlessly, and curtsied politely.

Mother had taught me always to say thank you. I reached out my fist, which was sore from pounding, and dropped the coin into the man's hand. Without objection, he complied with my request, although he did warn me to check the time in the future. Later I was teased about this early purchasing expedition when Nestor, laughing, told the story to villagers waiting for their mail in the store.

In those days, of course, the store was also a place for neighbors to congregate, chat, and analyze world events while waiting for the arrival of Postman Heikki, dragging his huge pack. Six days a week he fetched the mail from the post office in the church village. He made the twenty-kilometer trip pedaling a bicycle in the summer and pushing a kick sled in the winter.

Because Heikki's ramshackle bicycle always came down the road at a snail's pace, I once got the idea of speeding up the mail. Behind a clump of willows, I awaited the postman's coming with two rusty kettle lids in my hands. At the proper moment, I slammed the two implements together and let out an ear-piercing shriek. Heikki's bicycle did not launch into flight, as I had expected, but began to wobble from one side of the rocky road to the other, winding up in the ditch. When I peeped out from my hiding place, I saw Heikki crawling around in the ditch and grunting as he gathered up the scattered contents of his pack. I began to repent my action, for hadn't Mother always told me to respect old people? So I rushed out to help him. As payment for my assistance, Heikki brought Mother the news of my misdeed along with her mail. A flexible birch switch awaited me on my return home, administered with a stern warning that I was never again to frighten and humiliate innocent people.

"God always punishes such deeds," Mother said, concluding her sermon and the switching.

Afterwards I always curtsied deeply to Heikki on the road, hoping that the Heavenly Father would forget the matter and not drop hot stones on my head.

The God of my childhood was severe in his punishments. One had to repent and make amends in order to assure forgiveness. When in addition to a whipping, the threat of God's vengeance also loomed over one, it was wise to consider whether it was worth getting into mischief. Therefore, I did not join in the taunting of Fiina Taavi. It was mostly the boys who did that. "That kind of filth will land them in the fires of Purgatory," Grammy predicted gloomily.

Fiina Taavi was the most interesting person around chiefly because of her colorful language. She did not live in the community. No one knew for certain where her home was, or if she even had one. Fiina traveled the area spinning and carding for housewives. They liked her because she was a hard worker. She stayed in a house as long as she was needed, then went on her way. It was known that once in her youth, Fiina had made a "slip," and the result was a boy named Arvo. Nothing more was known about him. This was apparently a sore spot with Fiina, who never said anything about it. The boys found it a reason to tease her. Seeing Fiina on the village road, a flock of boys would run after her and sing: *"Arvon mekin ansaitsemme/Suomen maas-sa suuressa."* "We earn respect/ In this great land of Finland." Lines from a familiar song praising the virtues of Finns. The boys are punning on the word "arvo"/"respect" and the boy's name, Arvo, mocking Fiina for having "earned" him.

Then Fiina would turn around, spread out her arms, and let loose a torrent of words that would have made the most hardened lumberjack blush. I suspected that the boys taunted her in order to build up their own vulgar vocabulary. Otherwise Fiina was good-humored and liked to kid around. Sometimes when I was busy with my playmates outside, she would stop to stroke our hair and call us silly little piggies. In relating amusing events from her travels, she might use the same words she shouted in her rage at the flock of boys, but she spoke them tender-ly to us.

Fiina was talkative and gregarious. She stopped at our house often, although Mother could not give her any work. There was only one dwelling in the community in which she never set foot. That was Kalle Vertti's shanty. She did not like Kalle because he stayed at home while Sanna, his wife, went to work in the woods. Fiina berated him as lazy, and applied other names to him that would have gotten my mouth washed out with pine soap if Mother had heard me repeat them.

Other people too looked down on Kalle some-what, but Sanna saw nothing unusual in the situa-tion. In those days there was no talk of equality between the sexes. Sanna wielded a bark-peeling iron as well as any man, if not better. She was aware that the small and feeble Kalle was better suited to house-keeping. And it didn't seem to offend his manly honor. Along with keeping house, he also ran a business. He sold *korppua* (zwieback), good *korppua*—which had been liberally sprinkled with sugar and cinnamon. Once a week he got a sack of it from the bakery in the church village and then sold it to people in the neighborhood.

The couple also had a daughter named Liisa and a cat named Ivar. Kalle took care of them tenderly. He would prepare lunch for Sanna, and after she had set off with her peeling iron in her pack, he would heat some milk in which pieces of *korppua* were soaked and give them to Liisa and the tomcat. Ivar was indeed the community's fattest cat. Lissu too was round and red-cheeked. In the evening when Sanna returned, the coffee was ready in the copper pot. Sanna often boasted of all this when she was doing her shopping. But sometimes, when Kalle was a little tipsy and began to express his opinions in a group of men, Sanna would scold him gently:

"Be quiet, now, Kalle, and let the men talk."

I was brought back to the present by the voice of a young woman in the doorway, announcing to the world that the store was already open. I told the helpful clerk politely that I had found what I had come here seeking. There in the yard of that old store I had been able to travel in memory a stretch of my childhood village road and meet friends who had long since gone their ways.

Chapter Twelve

Kinkerit

The *kinkerit* was an annual reading examination conducted by the ministers of rural parishes in Finland.

It was an important winter happening in my home community in Pohjanmaa. Youngsters, especially, awaited it with a mixture of dread and excitement, for it was there that the provost of the parish tested aspirants to confirmation school for their knowledge of the catechism, and younger children for reading. Older people came too, to hear God's word. My first *kinkeri* experience made a particularly lasting impression on me because I had just learned to read. I did not haltingly sound out words from the ABC book, like some of my schoolmates in the first grade but could read real text from my big brother's reader. It was my devout wish to show off my brilliant reading skill to the provost and the *kinkeri* audience. But to my brother, who wanted to go to Confirmation School, the *kinkerit* and *Luther's Small Catechism* were a nightmare. He would study the catechism diligently every evening. I too tried to hammer the difficult text into my head and would question Pauli on it, with a great sense of gravity. In the process, the commandments stuck in my own mind. In time, all Ten Commandments went so smoothly that I expected the provost to be be amazed, and to heap praise on Pauli for his diligence.

Sometimes children were also brought to the *kinkerit* for baptism. Travel to the church village, especially during the winter, was often difficult, and thus people would wait till the provost came to their neighborhood for baptisms. That winter there were none. Only one child had been born, out of wedlock, to Saara Lampi, and it died after two days. Luckily Mari Mutka, who had been the midwife, was able to give the child an emergency baptism, so that its place in heaven was assured. Otherwise the poor soul would have been lost for all eternity, as we all knew. "It was a blessing that the poor thing left this cruel world," sighed Aliina Lindgreen, slurping coffee from her saucer while her other hand brushed a tear from the corner of her eye.

Earlier I had heard her condemning Saara to my mother for having a bastard child and bringing shame on her parents. A year earlier, Saara had gone to Helsinki to look for work. Soon afterwards, Aliina heard the news that things had gone badly for her. A wretch of a welder had led her astray. A married man. This news provided the women with gossip for a long time afterward, even when Saara, betrayed in love, had buried her child and returned to the great world.

Aliina was a masseuse. At the same time as she was massaging and cupping the ailing limbs of the villagers, she kept them informed of community events, distributed advice, and even scolded them when necessary. But she was not a mean person. Later she even lamented for Saara, wishing she would keep God in mind and no longer fall prey to the wiles of city dudes.

From that incident I learned the meaning of "bastard," and also understood why Taina Korpi would always run home sobbing when nasty boys hooted at her and called her by that name.

The *kinkerit* were held in the Heikkil house.

The big main room at Heikkils was filled to over-flowing with the *kinkeri* people. The adults sat on boards laid across saw horses, the confirmation children were arranged in rows on the window benches, and the children were in front on the floor. I wedged myself to the center of the throng facing the table, having decided that the provost would notice me there even if he didn't find my name in the book.

I was trembling with excitement when the pot-bellied provost, a skinny cantor at his heels, stepped into the room, and, with a dignified cough, settled himself behind the table. I had seen the provost in the pulpit of the church, from which he proclaimed God's word in a voice like thunder.

It was said that listening to his powerful voice kept the congregation awake. If anyone succeeded in closing his eyes, they were sure to pop open when he hammered the pulpit with his fist to give weight to his words. From close up, he looked even scarier. The Heavenly Father must look like that, I thought, when He drops that hot rock on my head.

The God of my childhood was angry and venge-ful, and we were always threatened with this rock when we were caught being naughty. Actually, I had begun to doubt the truth of the story, for to my knowledge no one had yet been clunked on the head with a rock. Not even Kassu Perala, who was always swearing, which was a worse sin even than lying. He sometimes had his hair pulled, even though he had not sinned. "He who spares the rod hates his child," the Bible says. In our family, children were not hated.

Loudly, devoutly, the *kinkeri* people sang "A Mighty Fortress Is Our God." Masseuse Aliina's shrill voice resounded over the roar. The pitch of her notes went its own way, but her words were bright and clear.

"God doesn't care about the notes as long as the words are clear," she would say in defense of her lack of artistry in song. After the hymn, there was a long sermon, in which the provost warned us to avoid temptation, which went around like a roaring lion, seeking whomever it could find to swallow. The questioning of the confirmation children began with Jenni Niemi. Hearing her name called, tall, thin Jenni strode swiftly up to the provost.

"What is most precious to us?" roared the voice from in back of the table.

"Most precious to us, Jennie said, in rapid reply, "is to come to know God and Jesus Christ, whom He has sent. He who knows God and Christ has eternal life."

Now Aliina will see how well Jenni knows the catechism, I thought with satisfaction. I knew that Aliina had publicly scolded Jenni, urging her to study her catechism, especially the Sixth Commandment. Aliina had heard that Jenni skipped off to dances and went around with boys. Everyone must have known that such evil conduct was not practiced before one had been to confirmation school. In those days it was an unwritten law that the gateway to such earthly pleasure opened only after confirmation school was completed and first communion enjoyed regardless of age. Jenni paid no heed to Aliina's scolding, but went her carefree way, dancing and caroling her sinful songs. Sometimes in the dusk of evening I would see her hastening to the community building, wrapping her thin coat more tightly around her, and piping in a shrill voice that trembled with cold, "Oh what cold hands are rapping at my breast." I remember wishing that Jenni could get a warm coat.

Jenni did not have to show her skill further, and then Pauli's name was heard. "How does the Fifth Commandment go?" asked the Provost.

Looking confused and shuffling his feet, Pauli answered hesitantly: "Thou shalt not kill."

"What does this mean?" thundered the shepherd of souls, raising his voice.

Scratching his ears as if trying to pry loose the knowledge stored in his head, the boy began slowly: "We should fear and love God that we may not hurt nor injure our neighbor in his body or spirit." Nothing more seemed to drip from the attic of memory.

Mumbling to myself, I sent him a message of the continuation: " . . . nor do we harm him, but help him in all perils and life's needs," but Pauli did not hear me.

The following candidates, stepping up in turn before the demanding gaze of the provost, came through without mishap except for the last one, Risto Koivu. He had studied Luther's Small Catechism no more diligently than he did his lessons at school, but he had an exceptional ability to improvise answers to questions that he did not know or understand. From Risto's copious flow of "Pig Latin" one could distinguish only a few words, but they sounded so convincing that a listener began to doubt his own powers of comprehension. The provost's question about how we were to treat our neighbors was barely out of his mouth when a flood of words poured from Risto's mouth, as if a dam had burst. In the breathless torrent, "eternal life" and "Christ's mercy" and other tag phrases flashed by occasionally. To conclude the incomprehensible litany, Risto whooped loudly,

"Don't oppress others, don't take hostages, don't rend or tear."

There was a sound of suppressed chortles from the audience; no one who would dare laugh in the provost's presence. That clergyman looked slightly confused as he dismissed Risto with a gesture. It may or may not be true, but it was said later that Risto was the only one in the history of the parish who was detained in his confirmation class and had to take it over again.

At last the reading tests began. Matti Pelto was the first, but the boy had barely sounded out half a verse from the hymnal when the provost snapped: "That's enough!" The same thing happened with the next three readers. *When he hears how good I am, he'll let me read a whole hymn,* I thought as I waited for my turn. It never came; there wasn't time enough for all of us.

When the provost called out Ville Ojala's name, I thought in disappointment that the provost should know that a pupil in the upper grades could read. When Ville had risen awkwardly, the provost did not order him to read, but instead asked: "Is your father still making whiskey?" An oppressive silence ensued, the only sound being the smacking of a winter-dazed fly into a windowpane. With a mixture of pity and sympathy, I watched as Ville blushed with shame and hung his head.

It was common knowledge that Ville's father, Jaakko Ojala, practiced this illegal manufacture to supplement the income of his large family. Being branded as the son of a moonshiner, Ville suffered from the mockery and hazing of his schoolmates.

Ojala's cottage was not in favor with the women-folk of the community because the men stopped there often for "coffee." The taste and potency of the coffee was in fact increased by the dash of joy-juice with which it was spiked. It cost one *markka* a cup. Jaakko also sold his product by the bottle. It was praised for being clear and potent.

If men tripping home from the cottage got disapproving glances from their wives and other narrow-minded citizens, nonetheless Jaakko's *markkas* eased the scanty living of the family. Those *markkas* were not easy to aquire.

He also had to be on guard in case a zealous, club-wielding policeman should appear to sniff out his stores. Once *Nisupoika*, the short, plump guardian of the law, succeeded in finding Jaakko's distilling equipment and smashing it until it was unfit for use. The menfolk had to wait a long time until the plant started up again, and coffee service was renewed at the Ojala cottage.

Finally the silence at the *kinkerit* was broken by the voice of Master Erkki Uusitalo, who stood up and announced in a firm tone of voice: "No he isn't. Jaakko is a fine man." It may not have been the whole truth, but when he heard the words, Ville raised his burry head and threw a look of gratitude at the upright master. The provost nodded approvingly, and began to read off the names of recently deceased members of the congregation from his register.

Later Aliina went on and on about it to her neighbors, asking if it were right that a servant of the Lord, who should have shown mercy to children, had shamed an innocent kid in front of everyone.

The long-awaited *kinkerit* concluded with the hymn, *Oh King of Kings*, ruler of heaven and earth . . . , and the great opportunity of my young life to demonstrate my skill ended with that closing hymn.

Chapter Thirteen

The Ski Race

This story happened during a time when Finland was at war with the then Soviet Union. Leather shoes for civilians were a rarity; even dresses were made of paper products. People had ration cards for the purchase of food, and farmers were not supposed to sell privately to consumers, but there was a black market, as the story makes clear.

The schoolyard rang with whooping and yelling and rapture. We were getting ready for the ski race. It was a big event, especially for the lower grades: for the first time we would be given prizes. All week long the boys had been zealously grooming the trail.

The course began at the edge of the schoolyard, crossed an open field, and wound along an old logging road. I had skied it once, taking good note of the hills, where I would have to be careful.

I was more afraid of breaking my skis than of falling. My grandfather had made them, and they were freshly tarred. My poles were smoothly scraped wooden shafts with horseshoe nails for points. The baskets were rings of twisted willow, with crossing strips of leather through which the poles ran. In addition to this extraordinary ski equipment, I had a new pair of ski boots, of which I was very proud.

Not many in the school had such fine boots. They had been bought with permission of the rationing board. The tops were actually real leather and the soles were of wood. My summer shoes also had wooden soles, but the tops were a paper weave and rubbed so badly my feet bled.

"You mustn't complain," scolded Mummo, when I showed her my sore feet. "The soldiers need the leather shoes when they have to chase the Russians."

Shoes were not really needed in the summer. The kids ran around on bare, chapped feet.

A group from the upper grades, who would race before us, gathered around their teacher at the edge of the field. The teacher was himself an avid skier, and was giving advice and help to those he considered the better skiers, especially those who brought honor to the school in competitions among the villages.

Their skis were waxed with real, store-bought wax. There was none of it left for those of us who were lower on the totem pole. I was happy with the stub of candle I had. With its help, I could glide to school in the morning, and with it I would make it through the race.

Kassu Perala came to a stop before me in a spray of snow. Leaning on his poles with the usual look of malice in his juniper-berry eyes, he asked sarcastically, "Ya think ya'll win a prize with those planks on yer feet, pruneface?"

I pretended not to hear, knowing that if his teasing went unanswered, Kassu would soon tire and seek a new victim. I also knew that my skis would go wherever his own store-bought skis, now patched with tin, would go.

Nor was I dreaming of winning the race, not even the second prize. A red pencil box with a yellow rose painted on its cover was the third prize, and that was my goal.

It was taken for granted that Taina Halme would win in my age group. She was a better skier, and her skis were factory made, with a rat-trap binding.

For my part she could keep her fancy skis, but her blue corduroy ski pants and poplin jacket turned me green with envy. I had to be content with a thick woolen dress with baggy woolen bloomers peeking out from under the hem. I had to wear them over my underpants in cold weather, and they were always threatening to slide down.

Stockings knit by Mummo kept my calves warm. Another pair, brightly striped, were neatly folded at the ankle over my boot tops. All this was crowned by my older brother's shrunken brick-red shirt and a knitted stocking cap.

"Even the best skier can't win in a get-up like this," I hinted to my father, telling him of Taina's finery in a voice that quivered with envy.

"She got them on the black market in exchange for butter," Father growled glumly.

"The devil will roast wrongdoers in hellfire," Mummo added in a voice of doom. She was a diligent student of Scripture, and if she did not approve of a deed, she always called on the Lord Zebaoth.

I didn't think trading on the black market was such a great sin, although it was against the law. I would willingly have traded my ration of butter and other card items for a pair of corduroy ski slacks. There was a shortage of food, and city-dwellers would pay practically any price for the agricultural products that Taina's Aunt Sophie smuggled to them.

Once that lady was shocked when officials pulled a surprise inspection of the bus she rode. Her butter and eggs were confiscated, and she was slapped with a fine as well. That didn't keep Sophie down. After a short layoff, she went on with her trade. Sometimes Taina accompanied her to town in the charcoal-burning bus, her poplin jacket bulging with hidden eggs.

To my relief, Kassu turned, and giving my rear a slap with his ski pole, disappeared into the hubbub in the yard. He was a constant pest, from whom I could expect almost anything whenever the teacher's back was turned. I had learned that, especially after I had succeeded in giving him a good thrashing for one of his tricks.

It still gave me pleasure to think of his squiggling in the ditch where I had pushed him, of the dust rising from his thick woolen pants as I lambasted him with a stick. He had paid me back for that humiliation many times over. I doubt that there was a cleaner face than mine in the school because he had scrubbed it in the snow so many times.

The upper grades were at the starting line, and the lower grades' instructor, leaflet in hand, was waving the others into line according to age. I could barely make out his face, blue with cold inside the collar of his lambskin coat as, shouting and threatening, he bounded around his flock.

It was obvious that our teacher was not interested in the ski race. At the head of the line, wearing a winner's expression, stood Taina. Thin, long-legged Pirkko Makela was behind her. I did mental arithmetic to figure out how many times my short legs would have to pump to match a few strides of Pirkko's. The second prize was hers, no doubt about it.

I could hear Kassu's hoarse cackle behind me. I had devoutly hoped that he would start ahead of me. Of course he'll pass me, I thought in a panic, and who knows what he'll do to harass me.

At the same moment I felt a nasty twinge in my stomach, and remembered that we'd been served lingonberry pudding in the school cafeteria that day. Thickened with rye flour and sweetened with saccharine, it was a tasty dish. I had once heard our teacher complain that Mrs. Kettunen, the school cook, did not let it finish cooking. Perhaps that was why I often had stomach trouble.

Everything was ready. The line began to glide forward toward the starting point. The teacher, a large pocket watch in his mittened hands, sent the racers off at even intervals. When I bounded off in turn, I had forgotten my troubles. Trembling with excitement, I darted across the field. My skis felt amazingly light, and the track gleamed a like a silken ribbon as it wound through the fir trees before me.

> When the gleaming snow
> covers the ridges,
> and the white frost
> coats all the trees
> then I strap
> my skis on my feet
> wrapping my jacket
> tight with a belt.

I caroled joyfully as, poles whistling and woolen pants flapping around my legs, I swung forward. There was no time to tug at my pants. I could barely manage to wipe off my dripping nose with the woolen sleeve of my shirt. About halfway, my pace slowed and the skis began to feel incredibly heavy, but the end of the logging road was already in sight. There the trail straightened out through the woods and rejoined the field. I tried to speed up.

As I puffed around the last turn in the woods, a spark of hope flashed in my mind. At this pace, I might take second place, since no one had passed me yet. Then I heard a shout behind me: "Track!"

I quickly skied to one side. Half of the trail was left for passing. That was the rule. "Out of the way, fatso!" rasped the winded Kassu, shoving me forcefully into the snow bank. Almost buried in snow, spitting it out of my mouth, voice shrill with rage, I screamed after him: "Piss pants, Piss pants!"

Struggling up from the soft snow, I kept on screaming, although Kassu had long since vanished from sight. For the first time I dared to make public his shameful secret. I knew that he still wet the bed.

When in tears I began to brush the snow from my clothes, to my horror I felt my insides contract sharply. Mrs. Kettunen's pudding and Kassu's villainy had produced such an upheaval within that I had to duck behind the nearest tree at once.

With the first stride, I sank waist-deep into the snow. It was useless to try to go farther. Disaster had already struck. I froze in place. Bitter tears of shame and rage began to drip into the snow. My honor and reputation were gone. The rest of the competitors skied by me. Not one of them wasted a glance at my wretched being. Fortunately. I wormed my way back onto the track and limped wailing on my way.

As I approached the finish, I saw that only the upper grades' teacher was still there. The yard was empty. They're in the warm classroom waiting for the awards, I thought bitterly. The chill wind began to blow through my woolen shirt. The pale sun of February was still sulking on the rim of the woods, but its rays were not enough to warm a suffering ski racer.

My tearful wailing had subsided to a shrill sniveling. I could no longer even dry the flow from my eyes and nose with my sleeve. It was shiny with ice.

Efforts to wipe my face merely spread the stuff around in a sticky mask. I made a wide and cautious circle around the waiting teacher and began to take off my skis.

"Don't cry, child," he consoled me in a kindly voice. "Next time you'll do better. Always remember, it's not winning that matters, it's that you do your best."

The answer to the sympathetic words was a new flood of tears. Sniveling, dragging my skis, I headed across the yard to the road, praying devoutly to the Heavenly Father to protect me on the way home, and not to let Kassu Perl cross my path.

Chapter Fourteen

The Flower Field of Memory

A choral concert of birdsong chimed out in the springtime grove of birch trees, sounding as if every warbler were competing to conjure up the sweetest melody. The sun's rays, filtering through overarching boughs, fell on a carpet of lily-of-the-valley, turning it into a glowing golden sea of flowers. Here and there a fading anemone thrust up its crown through the fragrant lilies, preparing to yield its place in the sun. I stood enchanted in the flower-fragrant grove and felt the chain of years glide by. For a moment I was young again.

Once more I was in my familiar lily-of-the-valley woods. I gazed at the slender trunks of the birches, wondering if they could be the same trees under which I had wandered gathering my favorite flowers, the same trees against whose trunks I had leaned as I listened for the call of the cuckoo. They were probably a new growth, but they were the same kind of birch under which I now sat to listen for the cuckoo's call. However, I did not hear the familiar note among the warbling flock. Still full of hope I decided there must be a cuckoo somewhere that would sense my devout prayer if I waited patiently. Yet I heard none.

When, disappointed, I rose at last to leave, a large crow flapped down onto the tree, and began a concert of ear-piercing caws. Tail feathers waggling, the bird peered down from the limb with its black button eyes as if asking if I liked its song. I wanted to believe that the drab-coated troubadour had sensed my hope and come in place of the cuckoo to cheer up a traveler from far away. A doubting Thomas would argue that his serenade was only an effort to lure a female from her hiding place in the grove, or was meant to drive an intruder from his nesting place. I believe otherwise.

A welcoming sauna awaited me. Thanking the crow, I bade farewell to the lily-of-the-valley woods and to the memories of my youth. Along with my friend, I waited for the sauna, a fresh birch switch, a dressing room decorated with rowan branches, with a bouquet of lily-of-the-valley on the table. It was the most beautiful, most welcoming sauna I have ever had in my life. I was deeply grateful, overjoyed to see my friend, to see springtime in the land of my birth again. My path had led me back many times, but the visits had always been brief, often hasty. Now I wanted to return for a time to the landscape of my childhood and youth and see a little more of my beloved Finland. My brother and his wife had come from Minnesota with the same intent.

A few days later, we began our journey in a rented Honda. Unhurriedly, enjoying ourselves, we breezed through the bright spring landscape, leaving the bustle of the highway from time to time for quiet side roads where we could find appealing lakeshore coves for rest stops. Sometimes we paused awhile in a pine grove fragrant with rowan blossoms to listen to the birds. Breathing in the scent of chokecherry blossoms at the roadside, we found their fragrance less intoxicating than songs claim. Or perhaps at our age our sense of smell was fading along with our memory.

Spring has always been my favorite season, but I experience spring more strongly in the country of my birth than anywhere else, perhaps because misty memories from one's early life, deeply embedded in our consciousness, lend a dreamlike cast to what we see there. We decided unanimously that only in Finland was the green of birches so marvelous or the sky so dazzlingly blue.

Along with the beautiful sights we were able to indulge our palates. Every coffee shop offered a supply of the world's best Danish and other baked goods. They added something extra to our journey.

As we approached the place where I had lived as a child, the villages seemed strange. Only the old church still stood, sturdy and solemn. In a niche in the bell tower stood the *vaivaisukko*, the wood-carving of the beggar with his hand outstretched for alms, but its paint was faded and flaked. The reminder on the upper part of the carving was also dimmer: "God has mercy on those who help the poor." The coin I dropped clinked hollowly in his apparently empty stomach. Modern society doesn't seem to need the old man to collect alms.

I remembered my father's old story of the bitterly cold day when he trudged the twenty kilometers to the church to drop a *markka* into the old man's bosom. Someone had shot the hated sheriff of the parish. That was worth an offering.

New houses and inhabitants had appeared in my former home town. Most of the familiar names I found were on gravestones in the cemetery. My childhood schoolmates had scattered to the four winds.

The best ski slope at Big Birch was still there at the edge of the village. Only the most reckless of daredevils would ski it from the top. On its slope, I broke the skis my grandfather had skillfully carved when Kassu Perl thrust the sharp point of his ski pole into my buttocks. That emboldened me to go flying down the slope myself. Now we climbed to the top of the hill and stood wondering at how oddly shrunken in size it was. Later we stood at the ruins of my childhood home. Dense spruce trees had taken over the open yard, but the white rose bush near the stone at the foot of the steps was a living link with the past.

All that was left of the well and its sweep was a heap of rocks sunk in a pit. When he had had a few drinks, Father used to sit on its cover playing his two-row button-accordion and singing to the neighbor women. After all these decades I can still see him in the summer twilight, accordion on his knee, head tilted to one side, hair hanging over his forehead, as he sang softly and mournfully:

> In a gloomy place deep in the forest,
> far off in the woods I was born.
> All we could hear was the sigh of the pines
> and the sound of the herdboy's horn.

The song tells of disappointments and shattered hopes on the road of life, and of a longing to return to a cabin in the woods. The women would dab at their eyes with the corner of their aprons, waiting devoutly for more.

> Left weeping were mother and sisters,
> my sweetheart was left all alone.
> The warm arms of my own true love,
> my joy and my happiness gone.

Father continued, a tremor in his voice. A tear probably rolled down his cheek too as the old accordion wheezed out the last sob. Longing, abandoned love, the pain of separation, were the major motifs of those summer evening concerts. It was just those themes that touched the listeners' hearts, revived old memories, perhaps brought a bit of romance into the gray routine of everyday life, and Father sang from the fullness of his heart.

We had an opportunity to go to the village's folk musicians' concert, and many a forgotten melody came back to me. To my delight, my ear picked up a few of Father's old threshing barn dance *polkkas* and *schottisches*.

There was uproar and clamor at those dances. Particles of soot fell from the roof and the dusty floor rumbled. As kids, we peered in through the black wall openings as Father beat time with his foot and played the lively strains of "Kottilas' wedding dance, where the bottles and flagons were waved. . . . " It was some shindig.

There are no longer any threshing barns, nor is the same kind of music played on the dance pavilions. The tempo has changed since my distant youth. Where once captivating waltzes and soulful tangos sounded, rock and roll now blares. However, "adult dances" are held, where one can do a turn in the old way.

Women's dances are also popular now. As one can conclude from the name, at these affairs, women are the choosers. Here the "crown of creation" can experience what it is like to be a wallflower, a fate which, I have heard, befell Artu, the bachelor owner of Ojala. He was no Adonis in appearance, but at dances he was a real planer of wood floors, and he was finicky about his dance partners. Only the young and shapely had the honor of gliding along on Artu's sturdy arm. Everyone knew that.

Once Artu decided to try his luck at a women's dance. Dressed fit to kill, he stationed himself in a conspicuous spot near the other males along the community building's open wall. Hardly had the accordion began to whine out the tempo of the first *humppa* when a colorful flock of female butterflies fluttered over to pick their partners.

Quickly men were snatched away to the left and right of Artu, but no inviting gesture came his way. Once he had already taken a couple of steps toward a blond gesturing toward him, but the invitation was meant for the large hulk of a man standing behind him. When it neared midnight and his luck did not improve, Artu shambled angrily home. In reply to the questions of the curious home folk next morning, Artu growled sullenly: "That's the last time I'll go there to be torn apart by women."

My brief sojourn along the path of my childhood ended with my brother's family heading north and my continuing my trip on the train. Train travel has also changed over the decades. Before, one had to jounce along for days on uncomfortable wooden seats on a trip that now takes only a few hours. The seats are comfortable and the coaches extraordinarily neat. Since I had last seen them, videos had made their appearance. Even long journeys transpire merrily when you are watching movies.

I chose a coach without this form of entertainment because I wanted to watch the scenery. At the window of the half-empty coach, I concentrated on admiring the landscape gliding by and mentally reviewing my experiences. In my mind's eye I surveyed the flower field of memory. There were many lovely memories there, bright and beautiful memories. Among them were thorns and nettles too, but the course of years has lessened their sting, and the daisies and brilliant bluebells shine brightly in the field of my memory.

I was awakened from deep in thought when a young mother with a boy of about five entered the train. The lively towhead was not content to sit near his mother for long, but began to trot along the aisle. He was not loud or intrusive but merely looked around with a lively curiosity. Like a wise little old man, he presented his observations to any traveler who prompted him.

Across the aisle from me sat a stern-faced gentleman. He stared straight ahead, paying no attention to the boy standing near him, who was eyeing the man's gleaming bald head with keen interest. Trying to catch the man's eye, with a touch of wonder in his voice, the boy announced in a bright voice: "Uncle, you don't have any hair."

There was not a flicker of expression on the man's stone face. For a moment the rascal stood there expectantly, then turned slowly on his heel, and with a final searching look at the man's smooth skull, said dryly: "Not a single goddamned hair."

The boy's clearly audible remark evoked snickers from the other passengers and brought the worthy gentleman to life. Angrily, he snatched his briefcase from the rack and stormed down the aisle to the next coach, his bald head glowing like the brake light on an automobile. When I left the train at the next station, I passed the little man on his seat, absorbed in a picture book, with his mother's arm wrapped tightly around him.

The nex day, I stood at the airport again, saying a poignant goodbye to my friends, in whose hospitable home I had begun and ended my journey. Beautiful memories remained with me. Waving Juha's beautiful bouquet of violets, I got on the plane, vowing that I would return.

768954   940 NA $7.95